ELEVEN AT No. 10

ELEVEN AT No.10

A personal view of Prime Ministers 1931-1984

by

Frank Longford

Harrap · London

FOR ELIZABETH

First published in Great Britain 1984
by HARRAP LIMITED
19–23 Ludgate Hill, London EC4M 7PD

© *Lord Longford* 1984

ISBN 0 245-54228-0

Designed by Robert Wheeler
Printed and bound in Great Britain
by Robert Hartnoll Ltd, Bodmin

Contents

Acknowledgments

As always, Elizabeth has provided the inspiration first and last. But the book would never have been written or achieved its present form, if it had not been for Harold Harris, wisest and most experienced of Editors. Gwen Keeble has been as invaluable as ever; Barbara Winch, my long-standing ally, Kitty Chapman and Matthew Oliver (who suggested the title) have given me indispensable help in preparing the manuscript.

Introduction

Introduction

DURING THE LAST HALF-CENTURY there have been eleven Prime Ministers, and I have known them all. To forestall complaints that this is inaccurate, since there have been twelve Prime Ministers, it is true that Ramsay MacDonald, whom I never met and have not dealt with in this book, did not finally resign until 1935. But he was only nominally Prime Minister in those last years. Baldwin, the leader of the vast Conservative majority in the National Government, had the real power, though he exercised it intermittently.

The book starts in effect in 1931, when the National Government was formed. Baldwin, who had been Prime Minister for the first time in 1923, and again from 1924 to 1929, formally took over from MacDonald in 1935. His third period of office lasted until 1937.

I suppose that I am the only Cabinet or ex-Cabinet Minister now living who has taught politics academically. When I was an undergraduate at New College, Oxford (1924–8) I took my degree in Philosophy, Politics and Economics. I taught in the same 'school' as a tutor at Christ Church (1932–9 and 1952–4). One of our basic papers in all these periods was called *Political Institutions*. I remember taking an essay to our Warden, H. A. L. Fisher, the illustrious historian and one-time Minister of Education.

I was asked to compare the powers of the British Prime Minister with those of an American President. Subsequently I set the same essay many times to students. The present book is not intended as any kind of academic text. I hope, however, that it will be of interest to those who teach and study politics, to those who practise the political arts and, of course, to the general public.

Since I began to work academically on these subjects, there have been cataclysmic changes in the world and far-reaching developments in Britain. Writing at the end of 1967, Humphrey Berkeley in a stimulating book argued that 'the basic defect in the British system of Government is the supra-presidential power of the Prime Minister'. But many passages in his book demonstrate that this can hardly be looked upon as a new phenomenon. 'The Head of the British Government', said Gladstone, 'is not a Grand Vizier. He has no powers, properly so-called over his colleagues; on the rare occasions when a Cabinet determines his course by the votes of its members, his vote counts only as one of theirs. But they are appointed and dismissed by the Sovereign on his advice. In a perfectly organised administration such, for example, as that of Sir Robert Peel in 1841–6, nothing of great importance is matured or would even be projected in any department without his personal cognizance and any weighty business would commonly go to him before being submitted to the Cabinet'. Berkeley admits that even as early as Gladstone's day the Prime Minister had become something more than *primus inter pares*. I doubt myself whether any Prime Minister in peace-time has possessed wider powers than Peel or Gladstone or Disraeli or used them more freely, though Mrs Thatcher may yet prove me wrong in the last respect. Today the domestic area covered by government is far wider than in the nineteenth century, as indeed is the patronage at the disposal of the Prime Minister. On the other hand, the reduction in Britain's international influence and the disappearance of the dependent Empire have diminished substantially the magnitude of the British Prime Minister's opportunities and burdens.

Let me take a quick look at the years from 1931 onward. Ramsay MacDonald was a leader only in name. Baldwin, who followed him, was very easy-going. From 1922 (when he first became Prime Minister) to 1937 (when he retired) he can never have been accused of exercising supra-presidential power, except in the sense that he enjoyed enormous popularity with the public. Chamberlain, who followed him, was his exact opposite – a dominant person given at last his chance to dominate. But he was not allowed much time to affect the institution. Churchill dominated the running of the war, but the home front and post-war planning – a huge area – was left to others. At all times he had to carry the Labour Party with him.

Attlee for six years after the war was in my eyes a great Prime Minister, but he worked through an inner Cabinet including such powerful, aggressive personalities as Bevin, Morrison, Dalton and Cripps. Eden made a disastrous attempt to run the foreign policy of the country on personal lines, but already a very sick man, he came to grief over Suez. Macmillan, though he told the Queen at the beginning of his term that his tenure might well be short, had become by the end the most dominant of all our post-war Prime Ministers before Mrs Thatcher arrived. His dismissal of seven Cabinet ministers at a stroke in 1962 may be seen as a supreme example of the excessive powers of the Prime Minister. It had always been understood that the Prime Minister can hire and fire, but this was surely overdoing it!

It is worth noting, however, that when Lord Kilmuir, the Lord Chancellor, was called to No. 10 Downing Street to be told about his dismissal Macmillan seemed to him to be obsessed by the dangers threatening his position. He had no doubt about his own vulnerability. I have been told that when he was invited to speak to the 1922 Committee (the Conservative back-benchers) he was kept waiting for an unconscionably long time in the corridor to teach him that he was no Oliver Cromwell. It is often said that the night of the long knives led to his downfall.

Of Wilson's premiership I can speak with more knowledge than others, as I was a member for three years of his Cabinet. (I often attended Attlee's Cabinet, however, as Minister of Civil Aviation and First Lord of the Admiralty.) It never struck me at the beginning of Wilson's Cabinet, or when I resigned from it on grounds of principle, or when it came to an end two years after that, that there was anything wrong about its procedure or anything excessive about Wilson's power or use of it. Certainly he adopted the methods of any effective company chairman with a view to getting business through in accordance with his ideas. Always the ultimate responsibility for a coherent result falls on the Prime Minister. I found that that was equally true in a much smaller way when I was chairman of a bank, and later of a publishing company.

I have never sat under a better chairman than Wilson. Any tendency to talkativeness on his part he sternly suppressed. He gave everyone a fair chance to speak (Barbara Castle perhaps being allowed a little extra latitude). In this respect he was possibly an improvement on Attlee, who could be somewhat abrupt and intimidating.

Just as Attlee in the last resort regarded Defence as his special subject, so Wilson for a long time would allow no discussion of the possibility of devaluation. It was 'the unmentionable', in Tony Crosland's phrase. But once we were pushed into it by circumstances, and Roy Jenkins took over the Exchequer, the economic policy was as much that of Jenkins as that of Wilson. After I had departed from the Cabinet, Wilson gave Barbara Castle enthusiastic support in her attempt to curb unofficial strikes. But the majority of the Cabinet defeated her and him.

When he formed his Cabinet in 1964 Wilson had only a bare majority in the House of Commons, and within his own Cabinet was in a lonely personal position. When he defeated George Brown for the leadership of the Labour Party eighteen months earlier it is said that only one member of his Shadow Cabinet voted for him. When I took my seat in the Cabinet and looked round at that 23-strong body I could only see four who could be regarded as Wilson men. All the time I was there Wilson had to work hard to carry the Cabinet with him. I used to reckon, however, that simply by virtue of his office he could probably count on six supporters if it came to a vote. Incidentally, many votes were taken, though it was sometimes called 'collecting the voices'.

Callaghan and Heath proceeded roughly on the same lines, Callaghan close to Wilson and Heath to Macmillan, though he never needed to use the long knives. Mrs Thatcher has asserted a form of personal rule which, coupled with a direct appeal to the masses, may seem a new departure. In the television age the personalization of the Leader is potentially greater, assisted by modern marketing methods. As against that, the decline of the large public meeting has deprived the demagogue of genius of a method of arousing enthusiasm for which television is a poor substitute.

After Mrs Thatcher had been in power for two weeks I jotted down in my diary the opinion that she wouldn't last more than two years. I reckoned that her colleagues would not stand her authoritarian methods for longer than that. In the event she solved her problem by getting rid of the dissidents. Whether she does or does not succeed in the long run, when, as Keynes said, 'we will all be dead', no one can take away from her the electoral triumph in 1983 after four years as Prime Minister.

The distinguishing feature of a Prime Minister's position is his capacity to hire or fire his so-called colleagues and transfer them from one post to another at a moment's notice. I can think of no parallel in other walks of life. I have mentioned above the massive changes in the personnel of the Cabinet effected by Harold Macmillan and Margaret Thatcher. But Neville Chamberlain treated individual colleagues just as ruthlessly. Eden as Foreign Secretary was humiliated to the point where resignation was the only honourable option. Lord Swinton was one of Chamberlain's three or four most significant colleagues, though he had (unwisely, perhaps) accepted promotion to the Upper Chamber. He was doing vital work in the strengthening of the Air Force. One fine day he was sent for by Chamberlain and told that he must leave the Air Ministry. He was offered another post, which he not surprisingly refused. Hore-Belisha, Minister for War, was treated in precisely the same fashion. He had been much less intimate with Chamberlain.

The insecurity of a Cabinet Minister (and it is still truer lower down) has to be experienced to be fully understood. When I was Leader of the House of Lords and a member of the Cabinet it was freely forecast that on reaching the age of sixty I would be 'chopped'.

The Prime Minister, Harold Wilson, was dangerously young from the point of view of my generation. He once said to me, 'Our trouble is that we are an old Cabinet. We are not only old, we look old.' He gazed at me benignly while saying this. What on earth was I to make of that? Was it a plain hint that my terminal date was approaching, or a rather subtle reassurance? I do not know to this day. But I cannot repeat too often that no Prime Minister can act like an oriental despot and get away with it indefinitely. In our democratic system his own insecurity matches that of his colleagues. This being so, I much doubt whether any movement to clip his wings will succeed. The immense responsibility falling on him is widely recognized.

No attempt is made here to describe the general development of British government during the last half-century. The development of the Cabinet committee system, including the appointment of *ad hoc* committees as desired by the Prime Minister, give him or her a range of options which may well increase the power inherent in No. 10. So may the strengthening of his or her personal staff or the Cabinet Secretariat or the creation of a Think Tank or its equivalent. But in my view the dominance or otherwise of a Prime Minister depends on more personal factors. On the one hand there is the Prime Minister's capacity and will to dominate, on the other hand there is the strength or weakness of his or her position *vis à vis* other members of the Cabinet. In the background there is the attitude of the Premier's political party. I feel sure myself that no Labour Party leader, Wilson, Callaghan or it may be Kinnock, will be allowed to be as authoritarian a Premier as have been the Conservatives, Chamberlain, Macmillan, Heath or Margaret Thatcher. The one party is ultra-democratic in tradition, the other prides itself on its respect for strong leadership.

It is my essential submission that the institution of Prime Minister has varied little if at all during the last half-century. But the use made of it by the Prime Minister of the day has varied, and will continue to vary widely.

Stanley Baldwin

The Lover of England

BALDWIN
Rt Hon. Stanley
(1867–1947)

M.P. (U) Bewdley Division of Worcestershire, 1908–37

Financial Secretary to the Treasury, 1917–21;
President of the Board of Trade, 1921–2;
Chancellor of the Exchequer, 1922–3;
**Prime Minister and First Lord of the Treasury, 1923–4, 1924–9
and 1935–7;**
Lord Privy Seal, 1932–4;
Lord President of the Council, 1931–5.
Created 1st Earl Baldwin of Bewdley, 1937.

The Lover of England

'WHY DO THEY hate me so?' asked Baldwin mournfully. As the war proceeded, the inadequacies of the British defence preparations became more and more glaring. The public turned desperately on the only scapegoat available, now that Chamberlain was dead. Baldwin bore it all with a kind of bewildered Christianity.

Stanley Baldwin's reputation, exalted at the time of his retirement in 1937, plummeted dramatically in the next three years. Today, when we try to view him dispassionately, we can still find contrasted opinions among those who knew him well. G. M. Trevelyan, the historian and Master of Baldwin's old Cambridge college, Trinity, said of him:

> Stanley Baldwin was an Englishman indeed in whom was much guile, never used for low or selfish purposes. In a world of voluble hates, he plotted to make men like, or at least tolerate, one another. Therein he had much success within the shores of this island. He remains the most human and lovable of all the Prime Ministers.

Austen Chamberlain, on the other hand, once wrote to his sister about Baldwin: 'Sly, sly, devilishly sly! would be my chapter heading and egotism and idleness the principal characteristics that I would assign to him.' One would hardly think that Trevelyan and Austen Chamberlain were referring to the same person. But Austen Chamberlain, the most honourable and usually the most fair-minded of men, could never get used to the idea that Baldwin was no longer the servant but the master.

Probably no one knew Baldwin better than Tom Jones, the Colonial Secretary, who served him and three other Prime Ministers. He recalls in his memoirs that the Swedish Ambassador once asked Mrs Baldwin whether she was a believer. She answered:

> I am indeed, and I must tell you that every morning when we rise we kneel together before God and commend our day to him, praying that some good work may be done in it by us. It is not for ourselves that we are working, but for the country and for God's sake. How else could we live?

Tom Jones considers that this was the truest clue to Baldwin's personality. I am sure he was right. It has become well known by now that he gave away a quarter of his fortune (derived from the family ironworks) to help diminish the National Debt. Many smaller acts of virtue are on record.

When I left Oxford in 1928 I used to be asked to stay in some grand houses. I was working in the Conservative Research Department, had got a first-class degree at Oxford, and was presumed to be a young man with a future. More than once I met Mr Baldwin as Prime Minister or as Leader of the Opposition. Neither of us could be said to have been completely 'at home', but he was naturally the centre of attention while I hovered about on the fringe. One Sunday afternoon, a guest of Lord and Lady Salisbury at Hatfield, I was told that Mr Baldwin wished me to go for a walk with him. I was flattered but surprised. He was not supposed to feel at ease with the young or with intellectuals of any age. He was understood to find Philip Kerr, later Lord Lothian, altogether too clever for him. He was often caricatured as dressed in tweeds, smoking a pipe and leaning over a pig-pen, studying the pigs, and referred to as Farmer Baldwin. Though I had been brought up in the country, and in Ireland my family had a large farm, I doubted my capacity to sustain a good conversation about either farming or natural beauty.

It may be that I was unduly anxious. Neville Chamberlain used to say with mild irritation that he himself was much more of a country-man than Baldwin. He fished and shot. Baldwin did neither. He knew every tree and flower, which Baldwin certainly did not. Yet Baldwin was always referred to as the countryman, he, Chamberlain, as the townsman. Baldwin, the much more countrified of the two in appearance, indubitably loved the country in the sense that he loved being in the country, and had an almost mystical feeling for the countryside. Lord Davidson has insisted that he really did like leaning over a gate and prodding a pig. I doubt, however, whether he would have wished to have a technical discussion of such matters.

As we made our way across the countryside the conversation lagged painfully. Only once, when I mentioned his son Oliver (at that time a Labour MP and supposed to have caused his family a lot of anxiety), did Mr Baldwin brighten. 'Dear fellow,' he exclaimed, coming to life suddenly. Then we trudged on again in virtual silence. Finally, as the house came in sight, I grew desperate. Somehow I must find out a little of the profound political philosophy with which I unquestioningly credited my leader. I informed him that I was teaching political theory for the Workers' Educational Association in the Potteries, and asked him, in full naïveté and with no shadow of irony, which were the political thinkers to whom he himself owed most. He reflected for a moment and then spoke quietly and emphatically: 'There is one political thinker who has had more influence on me than all others – Sir Henry Maine. When I was at Cambridge, his authority was complete and I never ceased to be grateful for all I learnt from him.'

I was, of course, all ears. After all, the walk had been anything but in vain. 'What', I persisted, as innocently as before, 'would you say was Maine's supreme contribution?' Mr Baldwin paused perhaps a shade longer and then said with conviction, 'Rousseau argued that all human progress was from contract to status, but Maine made it clear once and for all that the real movement was from status to contract.' He paused again, and this time for quite a while, and suddenly a look of dawning horror – but at the same time of immense humanity and confederacy – stole across his face. 'Or was it,' he said, leaning just a little towards me, 'or was it the other way round?'

I came away with a diminished respect for Baldwin the theoretician, but an undying affection for Baldwin the man. Nearly forty years later, as a member of Harold Wilson's Cabinet, though in a private capacity, I was deeply honoured to be invited to his neighbourhood to read one of the lessons at the celebrations of the centenary of his birth. I could feel his presence, though there was little in the way of visible memorial.

Stanley Baldwin was born in 1867, the son of a substantial Midlands ironmaster who became a Conservative MP and chairman of the Great Western Railway. His mother was a Macdonald of Celtic origin. Three of her sisters married men of distinction: the father of Rudyard Kipling; Burne-Jones, the Pre-Raphaelite painter and friend of William Morris; and Edward Poynter, a future president of the Royal Academy. She herself was a prolific author. Stanley went to Harrow, where he distinguished himself academically and athletically until a sad mishap occurred. He was caught with a piece of juvenile pornography. He had sent a specimen of his composition to his cousin at Eton, and was duly birched before breakfast by the headmaster. At Cambridge he enjoyed himself hugely, but his academic career was remarkable only for his steady decline. After getting a First in Part 1 of the History tripos he descended to a Second in Part 2. In the Finals he only managed to scrape a Third. 'I hope you won't have a Third in life,' his father wrote to him. That hope at least was fulfilled, though few third-class men can have attracted as much odium as Stanley Baldwin did during the war years.

He married Lucy Ridsdale, who excelled at cricket and hockey.

She is described by Montgomery Hyde in his admirable life of Baldwin as robust, cheerful, forthright and extrovert. When I came to know her she was distinctly stout but full of fun. I well remember her description of the lunch she gave for the delegates from the north and south of Ireland who had been invited to discuss the boundary between the two parts of the country. She put one group on one side of her and the other group on the other. She then remarked genially, 'I want you to imagine that I am the Irish boundary but I am too well covered to be a bone of contention.'

Stanley Baldwin worked away in the family business, developing very close relations with all employed there. By 1908 (already forty-one) he became Member of Parliament for his father's old seat. By 1917 he was Financial Secretary to the Treasury. By 1918, now over fifty, he was President of the Board of Trade and a member of the Cabinet, respected by all who had dealings with him but unknown to the general public. In 1922 he took the most decisive step in his whole career. He led the revolt against Lloyd George and the Coalition Government which caused its downfall. Baldwin was disgusted with what he regarded as the corruptness of the whole set-up. He was perfectly ready to retire if necessary into private life. In fact he emerged unpredictably as Chancellor of the Exchequer and a national leader. When Bonar Law collapsed he became Prime Minister.

A few months later he seemed to have thrown it all away. He suddenly espoused protection, and his Government was defeated at the polls. Nevertheless, by the end of 1924 he was back at Downing Street at the head of a large Conservative majority.

In the 1929 General Election he was thrown out for the second time, but by autumn 1931 he was back again in office as Lord President of the Council in the National Government. This, under the nominal leadership of MacDonald, meant Prime Minister in all but name. He became *de jure* Prime Minister in 1935 and won the General Election of that year and retired, acclaimed by all, in 1937.

Stanley Baldwin retired from the premiership on 28 May 1937. He had been Prime Minister for the first time in 1923, for the second in 1924, for the third in 1935. From 1931 to 1935 he was the dominant figure in the Cabinet presided over by the declining Ramsay MacDonald. He had been leader of the Conservative Party since 1923. No other retiring Prime Minister had ever left No. 10 Downing Street in a stronger glow of what Sir Winston Churchill has called 'public gratitude and esteem'. Yet within three years he was being execrated as no other British Prime Minister has ever been execrated. Baldwin bore it all with Christian resignation, though occasionally breaking out with an agonized cry, like that already quoted: 'Why do they hate me so?' The revolution in the public attitude is mercifully without parallel in our history. Stanley Baldwin had played no public part whatever between his glorification and his descent into the abyss.

The explanation is known to all of us who lived through that period. Between 1937 and 1940 Britain had come to find herself fighting for her very existence, in a conviction that her defences in the pre-war years had been scandalously neglected. The fact that this view had been repeatedly expressed in the years before the war by Winston Churchill, the new war Premier, made it certain that it would be generally accepted.

From the moment Churchill became Prime Minister he behaved with generosity to Baldwin as long as the latter lived. Baldwin died in 1947, but when the first volume of Churchill's war memoirs appeared in 1948, in the index occurred the notorious entry under 'Baldwin': 'Confesses putting Party before country, pp. 169–170.' Authors do not always give their index their personal attention. But if one turns to the pages in question and other passages, they are scathing enough. Churchill quotes the all too memorable speech of 12 November 1936, in which Baldwin explained his reasons for not promoting rearmament much sooner. He used the unhappy words: 'I cannot think of anything that would have made the loss of the election from my point of view more certain.'

It is understood today that Baldwin was referring not to an election in 1935, but to one that might have taken place earlier. Be that as it may, Churchill comments in his war memoirs:

> This was indeed appalling frankness. It carried naked truth about his motives into indecency. That a Prime Minister should avow that he had not done his duty in regard to national safety because he was afraid of losing the election was an incident without parallel in our Parliamentary history.

Churchill is at pains to deny that he is accusing Baldwin of any ignoble motive, but the general impression he leaves is not unfairly represented by the reference already quoted in the index. Churchill incidentally considers that the major damage had been done by the end of 1936, though a partial rescue was still possible. It is 1931–5 which he calls 'the locust years'. Of them he writes: 'We must regard as deeply blameworthy before history the conduct not only of the British National and mainly Conservative Government, but of the Labour-Socialist and Liberal parties, both in and out of office, during this fatal period.' Baldwin, who was (or if he had done his duty should have been) the effective head of the National Government during those years, qualifies by implication as the prime scapegoat.

There has been a good deal of writing about Baldwin since that time. The authorized biography by G. M. Young turned into a hostile tract. Baldwin's younger son, Wyndham, made a gallant attempt to defend his father, for which anyone who admired the father and the son will always be grateful. There have been two comprehensive biographies: that by Middlemass and Barnes runs to eleven hundred pages, that by Montgomery Hyde, one of the ablest of contemporary biographies, nearer to six hundred than five hundred. Any serious student will obtain from these comprehensive volumes a fair appreciation of Baldwin's personality and total achievement. But the Churchill view of his failure to rearm the nation during the crucial years is unlikely to be overcome. On the death of Baldwin a first leader was published in *The Times*, most of it written by Tom Jones.

> Our unpreparedness for war was blamed on him alone; posterity will be more just, but it is certain that the man who was thrice Prime Minister between the French occupation of the Ruhr and the visit of Chamberlain to Munich will have to bear a large share.

But is the nature of our criticism to be political or moral or both? To quote a shrewd analysis by his son:

> There are two aspects of criticism to be seen. There is the censure on deeds and the censure on character, and the latter is by far the more serious. Some of the critics attack the two together, and it is often hard to distinguish between the one and the other.

I will take the latter criticism first. His son tells us in poignant terms of his father's later sufferings:

> The fight was one for himself alone and involved a kind and degree of suffering beyond anything he had known before: suffering far worse than the fear of death, to see his long high-built honour plucked down in mock and to know that he would never live to see it restored. He never ceased to say and try to feel 'Thy Will be Done' but that side of his nature he did not attempt to use in public apologia.

How could it be, however bitter the resentment about the failure to rearm the nation, that someone so exceptionally honourable should be denigrated in this fashion? Other Prime Ministers – Lloyd George, for example – have been plausibly accused of being too clever by half. But Baldwin! Surely there is no justice in the world which impugns *his* honour.

The explanation may be sought in the eulogy already quoted by

G. M. Trevelyan, the historian and Master of Baldwin's old Cambridge college, Trinity. 'Stanley Baldwin', said Trevelyan, 'was an Englishman indeed, in whom was much guile, never used for low or selfish purposes. The phrase "much guile" used in an oration of this kind can be reasonably translated to mean "rather deceitful".' Politicians accept a certain amount of guilefulness as a not discreditable feature of their profession. Churchill in a generous panegyric described Baldwin as 'the most formidable politician I have ever known'. The point about Baldwin was that he was capable of blurting out thoughts and calculations that other guileful politicians kept to themselves. It often paid off, but when things went wrong it did him infinite damage. But there was a deeper consideration. Baldwin was regarded above all as Honest Stan. Even if the general public were left with the general impression that he was no worse than the others, he appeared to be presenting himself as someone better. One must repeat, however, that anything he did or said was done or said by the time he retired, and at that moment he was acclaimed by everyone. It was the disasters that followed which produced the retrospective denunciation. So much for what might be called the moral criticism. No honest student today would regard Baldwin as other than an honourable man.

But morality is not the only element in statesmanship. How far can we accept the *political* defence of Baldwin's statesmanship in the years 1931–7? Was it impossible for him to lead the nation into rearmament much earlier and more vigorously? Some weight must no doubt be given to the contention that he was badly informed. No doubt it is also true that no statesman of that period had any idea how long it would take to rearm Britain adequately. But, going deeper, we must attend to the quotation from Hegel which Barnes and Middlemass place at the beginning of their comprehensive work:

> The great man of the age is the one who can put into words the will of his age, tell his age what its will is, and accomplish it. What he does is the heart and essence of his age; he actualises his age.

Baldwin was not likely to be interested in Hegel. Political theory was definitely not his subject, as indicated above. Nevertheless, the quotation from Hegel must be thought significant, placed where it is by two academic authors soaked in a study of Baldwin. The passage quoted suggested that a leader must reflect public opinion. He can only guide it within narrow limits, and this is surely close to Baldwin's attitude.

Baldwin was not always a passive leader. On more than one

occasion he led the way boldly towards peace in industry. He ran every possible risk when he supplied the crucial leadership in the direction of Indian independence. But in each of these cases, though he defied large elements in his own party, he could feel that he was expressing the 'real will' of the British people as a whole, though that phrase would have been too reminiscent of Rousseau and Hegel to appeal to him. There was no such underlying 'real will' in favour of rearmament in the thirties. Except in the most abstract sense, the real will at that time was for keeping our head well under the bedclothes from which Stanley Baldwin made no attempt to extract us.

Baldwin had another limitation which might be said to be characteristic of many Englishmen, but was nonetheless fatal during the locust years. There is no escaping the fact that he was indifferent to foreign affairs. Lord Home puts his finger on one aspect of this. 'Baldwin had one weakness, he was ill at ease with foreigners and used to go so far as to contrive that he need not sit next to them at meals.' 'We must get nearer to Germany,' he told Eden, the Foreign Secretary, in May 1936. 'How?' asked Eden. 'I have no idea,' was the reply, 'that is your job.' When Chamberlain became Prime Minister he said to Eden, 'I know you won't mind if I take more interest in foreign policy than S.B.' 'We both knew', wrote Eden afterwards, 'that no one could have taken less.' It will have been noticed above that Trevelyan carefully said of him, 'He had much success within the shores of this island.' In his earlier years of leadership it might not have mattered. But here was a deadly weakness once Hitler had come to power in Germany.

The other alleged errors of commission and omission are essentially three: 1) Germany should have been held down indefinitely. 2) On the other hand, we should have taken Germany much sooner into the comity of nations on a basis of friendship and equality. 3) We should have been faithful not in words only, but in deeds, to collective security.

The first charge, even though propounded by Sir Winston himself, is quite simply ridiculous. Who seriously supposes that we could have held down the Germans for ever? In the first volume of his war memoirs, Sir Winston describes his underlying theme in this way: 'How the English-speaking peoples through their unwisdom, carelessness and good nature allowed the wicked to rearm.' The volume appeared in 1948. Even by that time it must have seemed an anachronistic doctrine. I describe later on a meeting with Winston Churchill at Buckingham Palace in 1947. I was aware from then on that he saw Germany as a future partner who must be raised up to an eventual equality.

The other criticisms, that Baldwin failed to work for friendship with Germany and give genuine support to the League of Nations, are valid enough. His minimal interest in foreign affairs explains his conduct all too readily.

Baldwin has been called a 'healer' by Harold Wilson. His love of his fellow-countrymen – most of them when he met them, all of them in the abstract – fitted him perfectly for this role within his homeland. His healing outside Britain was negligible – with one striking exception. When the whole history of Indian independence is written, the first British name must always be that of Attlee; but Baldwin should be reckoned a good second. His speeches on India in the thirties were perhaps the noblest he ever delivered, all the more because of the powerful opposition of Churchill and other strong influences in his own party. How much his friendship for Halifax, then Lord Irwin and Viceroy, extended his vision for once outside his own country one cannot say. Whatever their emotional origin, they can take their place in any national anthology.

One quotation must serve to illustrate his tone and style:

> Nobody knows what Dominion status will be when India has responsible government, whether that date be near or distant, but surely no one dreams of a self-governing India with an inferior status. No Indian would dream of an India with an inferior status, because that would mean that we had failed in our work in India. . . . We politicians . . . so much of our fighting is in the twilight, or in the mist – pass away before we know the result of our work. Our work must be done in faith, but let us build for the future with the same faith that we work for the present, so that when perhaps, in long generations to come, there are men who will be putting the coping-stone upon this building, they may not be unforgetful of those of us who built in faith among the foundations.

Attlee said in the House of Commons at the time of Baldwin's death: 'I always felt myself, when he was speaking, that although he disagreed with us, he understood better than any man on the other side the reasons and emotions that inspired our actions.' Attlee said the same thing to me in more intimate terms in the tea-room of the House of Lords: 'He used to like talking to our fellows, particularly the miners in the smoking room. Seemed to prefer them to his own side.' In this and other respects, Attlee drew a comparison between Baldwin and Chamberlain disparaging to the latter.

I decline to believe that any of this was artifice. It was quite a dangerous line for Baldwin. In his fifteen years' reign as leader of the Conservative Party he was more than once on the edge of a precipice. Heaven knows how he would have fared in these days of instant popularity polls.

His worst moment came in the spring of 1931. The pressure against him from Conservative circles, not created by but very much stirred up by the press lords Rothermere and Beaverbrook, escalated to the point where it hardly seemed possible for him to survive. When Neville Chamberlain told him that it was the general view of his principal colleagues that there should be a change of leader he said: 'Very well, the sooner the better, Let's have a meeting of my colleagues tomorrow morning when I can say goodbye.' His old friends, Davidson and Bridgeman, walked over after dinner to Upper Brook Street where they found the Baldwins 'quite convinced that they were about to retire from politics altogether and retreat to their home in Worcestershire where they looked forward to a period of complete leisure'. They also spoke of cutting down their living expenses, and even of selling the Astley estate. 'Well,' Lucy Baldwin greeted the visitors, 'we four were together at the beginning of Stanley's leadership and now we're together for the farewell.'

'Farewell be damned,' said Bridgeman. There was a by-election due at St George's, Westminster. Bridgeman persuaded Baldwin to fight St George's himself in order to challenge the right of the Press millionaires to dictate procedure to the party. Chamberlain, when told of this decision, was horrified: 'S.B., you can't do that.'

'Why not?'

'Think of the effect on your successor.'

Baldwin replied curtly, 'I don't give a damn about my successor, Neville.' As Churchill once wrote of Asquith, he did not rely entirely on rose-water.

In the event, Duff Cooper came forward as the Conservative candidate. He performed with much courage and eloquence, and won a magnificent victory which destroyed the open opposition to Baldwin.

He himself, however, was perfectly ready to fight the by-election, and would surely have triumphed from his favourite jumping-off ground – the last ditch. In the event he humiliated Beaverbrook and Rothermere with infinite gusto in a classic diatribe. He finished with a phrase suggested by his cousin Kipling: 'What the proprietorship of these papers is aiming at is power, and power without responsibility – the prerogative of the harlot throughout the ages.'

Baldwin's supreme weapon was his oratory, already illustrated in the case of India. Chamberlain referred to him without notable enthusiasm as a poet. He was certainly an artist who relied much more on a rapport with his audience than any other twentieth-century orator, with the possible exceptions of Lloyd George and Aneurin Bevan, both Celts. Baldwin's special gift was often attributed to the Celtic blood on his mother's side. His strange, nervous gestures may have sprung from the same source. I remember his giving me a physical demonstration of what it was like when 'you know you've got them'. With a smile on his face, he passed into a kind of mobile trance. Each year he seems to have exhausted himself so totally by the end of the session that a long holiday in Aix was essential. Just before and just after his last year in office we are told that he underwent a nervous breakdown.

He was full of sentiment about England. Again one quotation must do for the rest. Speaking to the Peace Society in the General Election of 1935, he suggested that

> we avert our thoughts from these terrors and send them roaming over this 'dear, dear land'. We think perhaps of the level evening sun over the English meadow with the rooks trundling noisily home into the elms; of the ploughman 'with his team on the world's rim creeping like the hands of a clock', one of those garnered memories of the long peace of the countryside that a wise man takes about with him as a viaticum. To what risks do we expose our treasures, for you cannot build up beauty like that in a few years of mass production? Make no mistake: every piece of all the life that we and our fathers have made in this land, every thing we have and hold and cherish, is in jeopardy in this great issue.

What Prime Minister but Baldwin could have written this about the Eton and Harrow match: 'There go the boys eternal. And there never to be forgotten are the little sisters, most loyal of comrades in weal and woe.' It is rather an anticlimax to recall that Baldwin (like Churchill, who loved to sing the old songs of Harrow) sent his sons to Eton.

The most famous of all his perorations ended with the words: 'Give peace in our time, O Lord.' The speech was delivered in the critical months before the General Strike.

Harold Wilson has stated with some justification that in the end Baldwin 'sold out to the mine-owners'. Yet the atmosphere he created left a fundamental goodwill towards him throughout the trade-union movement.

Beyond question his handling of the Abdication was masterly. Certainly it raised his popularity to a new height. The Duke and Duchess of Windsor were left, not surprisingly, with sour memories of Baldwin, but he must have been consoled by the handwritten letter from Queen Mary, who had heard him tell the whole story in the House of Commons the day before. 'We all listened to your wonderful speech yesterday and I feel I must write and thank you for the kind way you spoke of the King . . . thank you gratefully and with all my heart for the kindness and patience you have shown towards the King during these anxious weeks.'

Harold Nicolson in his diary for 10 December 1936 gives us a memorable glimpse of Baldwin. He bumped straight into the latter in the corridor of the House of Commons immediately after his triumph. No one, says Nicolson, 'has dominated the House as he dominated it tonight, and he knows it'. However, his comments were unpredictable. Referring to Edward VIII, he said, holding Nicolson by the arm, 'The man is mad, mad. He did not realize that any other considerations prevail. He lacks religion. I told his mother so. I said to her, "Ma'am, the King has no religious sense."' Then to Nicolson with a Baldwinesque touch: 'I suppose you are either an agnostic or an atheist, but you have a religious sense. I noticed it the other day.' Nicolson apparently had stood up for Ramsay MacDonald. He suggested to Baldwin that Winston, whom Baldwin had just described as 'the most suspicious man I know', had put himself in a false position. Baldwin flung up his hand: 'We are all in false positions.' If Baldwin had not existed it would not have been possible to invent him.

It cannot be said that Stanley Baldwin laboured ceaselessly for the public good. There was a strain of indolence – connected, perhaps, with his tendency to nervous exhaustion – which was never overcome, and he had a strange, detached sense of humour. On one occasion everyone in the House of Commons was waiting for the result of a crucial by-election at Rotherham. An MP brought in a slip of paper and handed it to Baldwin, sitting on the front bench. The Rotherham by-election result, he announced excitedly. Baldwin became reflective, dropping the piece of paper on the floor. 'Rotherham,' he said reminiscently, 'I remember once changing trains at Rotherham. They had square seats in the station lavatories. Someone had scribbled up on the wall:

> If square seats don't bother 'em,
> They've got rum bums in Rotherham.

He kept on murmuring the words to himself. All interest in the Rotherham by-election had passed him by.

But when a crisis was placed in front of him he knew only one answer, which was to put self entirely aside and act according to moral inspiration only. So it was when he destroyed the Lloyd George coalition, when he pleaded for peace in industry, when he defied and routed the press lords, when he took second place in a National Government of which he could so easily have been the leader. Baldwin, for all his highly strung sensibility, was a tough opponent. Those who bumped against him came off worst. As Churchill has been the first to acknowledge, and as Lloyd George,

Beaverbrook and Rothermere found to their cost. If the curse of Hitler had not fallen on the world he would have gone down in history as one of our greatest Prime Ministers. As it is he will assuredly emerge as an astute but also inspiring leader of men. When they turned against him he was able at much cost to say to his Maker, 'Thy will be done.'

Neville Chamberlain

The Chief Executive

CHAMBERLAIN
Rt Hon. (Arthur) Neville
(1869–1940)

M.P. (U) Ladywood Division of Birmingham, 1918–29;
Edgbaston Division, from 1929.

Director-General of National Service, 1916–17;
Postmaster-General, 1922–3, and Paymaster-General, 1923;
Minister of Health, 1923, 1924–9 and August–November 1931;
Chancellor of the Exchequer, 1923–4 and 1931–7;
Prime Minister and First Lord of the Treasury, 1937–40.

The Chief Executive

NEVILLE CHAMBERLAIN WAS before all else a Chamberlain. He was very proud of his family, and very sentimental about it. On 4 February 1932 – 'the great day of my life', as he called it to his sister Hilda – he unfolded the proposals for a general system of protection to a crowded House of Commons. When he came to the peroration of his speech his voice began to falter with emotion. He had difficulty in controlling it. He said:

> There can have been few occasions in all our long political history when to the son of a man who counted for something in his day and generation has been vouchsafed the privilege of setting the seal on the work which the father began but had perforce to leave unfinished. . . . I believe [he continued with ever more visible feeling] my father would have found consolation for the bitterness of his disappointment if he could have foreseen that these proposals, which are the direct and legitimate descendants of his own conception, would be laid before the House of Commons, which he loved, in the presence of one and by the lips of the other of the two immediate successors to his name and blood.

I can think of no close parallel to this extreme of filial piety in modern times.

Winston Churchill's father left an unfinished life, to which Churchill paid ample tribute in his massive biography, but he never claimed in his days of glory that he was finishing the work of Lord Randolph, who had after all resigned in the hope of keeping down the naval estimates. In my early days in the House of Lords, the dominating figure was the Lord Salisbury of the day ('Bobbity'). His great-grandfather, grandfather and father had all been Leaders of the House of Lords. His grandfather, the Prime Minister, is the main figure in the picture in the corridor of the House of Lords throwing out the Home Rule Bill of 1892 by an overwhelming majority, although it had been passed by the House of Commons. His father's bust was close at hand; but I cannot visualize Bobitty Salisbury speaking about his family so emotionally in public, although no family, not even the Chamberlains, could have felt a greater pride of ancestry.

The point about the Chamberlains was that they were supreme

throughout a large central area of Britain. They were in that sense regional aristocrats, though titles in the ordinary sense were not for them. In the last hundred years the House of Lords has seen the arrival of many successful businessmen, but there have been no Chamberlain peerages. When Chamberlain was dying Churchill, 'with the King's willing assent' (says Montgomery Hyde), offered Chamberlain the Order of the Garter, which would of course have made him 'Sir Neville'. But this the dying man respectfully declined, as he had previously refused to accept a peerage, preferring – as Churchill later told the House of Commons – 'to die, like his father, plain Mr Chamberlain'. Austen Chamberlain became Sir Austen KG, but as will be pointed out in a moment, he was a less typical Chamberlain.

It should be mentioned here that belonging to the Chamberlain family did not necessarily mean being called Chamberlain. The Chamberlains supplied the leadership to a far-reaching network of family relationships in the Birmingham area. When Neville Chamberlain became Lord Mayor of Birmingham in 1915, at the age of forty-five, he undoubtedly owed much to the family connection. Five of his uncles and ten other relatives had already held the office. Their pre-eminence in business and local government was quite extraordinary. Neville Chamberlain had exceptional opportunities, and availed himself of them to the full.

In later days he was often praised, correctly, as a model of efficiency. It is worth being reminded by his official biographer, Keith Feiling, that he was in those days in Birmingham a model of persuasiveness and conciliation. 'He should have been a Labour man,' was said on those benches. But to quote Dr Feiling: 'A business city respected his business powers.'

It is impossible not to think of Neville Chamberlain as a supreme bourgeois, embodying the virtues and weaknesses of that ill-defined if meaningful category. From the day when Joseph Chamberlain left the Liberal Party (1886) and gradually coalesced with the Tories, there has always been a tension within the Conservative Party between the aristocratic and the middle-class traditions. When Lord Cranborne (as he then was, later to be Lord Salisbury) resigned from Chamberlain's government along with Anthony Eden in 1938, he received a congratulatory telegram from his uncle, Lord Cecil of Chelwood (Lord Robert Cecil): *A bas les bourgeois*. So it has continued. The Conservative Party was led by three successive businessmen, Bonar Law, Baldwin, Chamberlain, then by four aristocrats, Churchill, Eden, Macmillan (harder to label, but married to a duke's daughter), Home. Since then, Heath and Thatcher have emerged from the lower middle class, as distinct from a family such as that in which Neville Chamberlain grew up. It would be a mistake, however, to think of Neville Chamberlain as the only possible embodiment of the Chamberlain tradition. As in all families, there was plenty of variety. But it does seem to me that Chamberlain gained much of his strength from his pride of family, and that at the same time it narrowed him down and increased what may have been in any case a natural tendency to intolerance.

My own recollections of him are possibly a trifle jaundiced. From 1930 to 1932 I worked in the Conservative research department. Neville Chamberlain became our chairman. We were a small group, the director Joseph Ball and four research officers. One of these was Henry Brooke (later Lord Brooke, and a Cabinet Minister of integrity and solid merit). Another was Henry Stannard, born Steinhardt, a small, very brilliant man of Jewish extraction from Chamberlain's Birmingham. He had made his way to Oxford, achieved many successes there including the presidency of the Union, but had not quite succeeded in life. He supplied a valuable satirical element in our ultra-serious little society.

He told me one story of his youth to illustrate the worship extended to Joe Chamberlain at that time in Birmingham. He himself was invited by the President of Magdalen to a reception given to the illustrious Joe on a visit to Oxford. It was a moment of supreme opportunity for this humble product of a Birmingham school (King Edward's). Who knew what benefits it might bring him? But when the time came his knees knocked together. It was too much like encountering God. He begged to be excused. He preferred not to meet Mr Chamberlain. By the time I knew him, however, he had lost such inhibitions.

I will tell the story of one of the visits Neville Chamberlain paid to our room on the third floor of Old Queen Street, overlooking St James's Park. The visit was quite unexpected. When Joseph Ball threw open the door and announced with some *empressement*, 'Mr Neville Chamberlain', there was a moment of flap from which Stannard recovered long before I did, in spite of having to conceal a French novel rather imperfectly. Neville Chamberlain showed every desire to put us at our ease. In a dead silence he walked over to the window, gazed across the park for a moment, appeared to be thinking hard for something to say, and then threw out the gambit: 'I wonder if those trees are cherry trees?' Stannard drew himself up to his full five feet three inches. 'All trees', he remarked in his old-fashioned Union manner, 'are cherry trees.' Chamberlain looked at him, puzzled. 'Surely', he said, 'that's rather an exaggeration.' 'All truth', said Stannard still more pontifically, 'is an exaggeration.' Chamberlain seemed to ponder this one deeply. He frowned, less it seemed in rejection than in genuine bewilderment. He left the room with no further word spoken on either side, and never visited us upstairs again.

It is no good pretending that Neville Chamberlain was interested in us as individuals, but he was concerned about our welfare, most genuinely. I remember being bidden to his room (this only happened to me twice). He asked me some trivial question which arose out of a document of mine. But what he really wanted to know was how Stannard felt after a recent accident.

Neville Chamberlain's daughter, Dorothy, was one of the brides-maids at my wedding, as a cousin of my wife's. It was a big, expensive affair at St Margaret's, Westminster. All working in our small office, including the secretaries, were very excited, and I know that they much enjoyed the occasion. But they received a message, at what point I am not quite sure, that Mr Chamberlain would be returning to the office, so that they also must return, missing the reception. It should be recalled, in fairness, that this was a week after the General Election. He had just become Chancellor of the Exchequer, and was phenomenally hard-pressed. Nevertheless, I felt that his powerful family feeling had stopped short of me, not to mention my wife, his first cousin once removed.

My experience with Austen Chamberlain was curiously different. He and his wife were great friends of the Birkenheads, a family with which I had become intimate. When I was writing my book on the Anglo-Irish Treaty Austen Chamberlain out of the goodness of his heart offered to let me read his own diary for the relevant period (October–December 1921). Later, I developed qualms. I wrote to tell him that my conclusions might be unpalatable to him. He wrote back, generous as always, and said that he would nevertheless *read* to me the notes in question, which he duly did, to the great benefit of the book. At the end he told me, in the kindest way possible, 'I much respect the feeling that prevented you reminding me that you are my cousin.' So family feeling can express itself in different ways.

Austen and Neville Chamberlain were much attached to each other, though on the face of it two men could hardly have been more different. Austen Chamberlain, with his monocle, striped trousers and perfect French, was every film-maker's idea of a Foreign Secretary or Ambassador. Lloyd George once referred to Neville Chamberlain as 'a competent town clerk of Birmingham in a lean year'. It was a ludicrously unfair assessment, but the appearance of Neville Chamberlain – nicknamed by Brendan Bracken 'The coroner' – gave it enough verisimilitude to raise a laugh. He was sometimes described as 'corvine' in aspect, but I must be careful of disparaging his looks. Soon after my eldest son Thomas was born my wife told Neville Chamberlain at a house party of the Astors at Cliveden that Thomas, a few months old, resembled him (Thomas was his first cousin twice removed). Neville accepted the news calmly. 'It's a very strong strain,' he remarked contentedly.

The difference between Neville, born 1869, and Austen, born six years earlier, can be partly attributed to the contrast in their training. Both went to Rugby, but Austen was sent on to Cambridge with a view to a big career in politics, culminating presumably in the premiership. Much assisted by family influence, he became Chancellor of the Exchequer in 1903 at the age of forty. Neville was extremely unhappy at Rugby. A friend urged him to speak in the debating society of which he was a silent member. Neville vehemently replied:

> No, I don't take any interest in politics, I never shall. . . . You don't know what our house is like for days before my father makes one of his big speeches. Everybody has to be quiet and even at meals conversation is subdued. . . . Wretched man, he never knows what he is going to say.

Despite this surprising outburst, his devotion to his father stopped not far short of idolatry.

After leaving school he was destined for a career in business. For some years he managed a plantation in the West Indies in which heavy losses were incurred through no fault whatever of his own. He was left with a heightened determination to bring fresh honour on the family name.

In his own environment of Birmingham he soon made his mark in local government and business. He became chairman of a firm manufacturing copper, brass and yellow metal. He also ran an engineering firm, Austin & Sons, producing 'metal fabrications'. In 1911, aged forty-two, he was elected to the Birmingham City Council. By 1915 he was Lord Mayor, able to point to many municipal achievements. In 1917 he was appointed Director of National Service by Lloyd George, a new post for mobilizing the nation's manpower. The terms of reference were vague. Without a seat in Parliament, let alone a ministerial position, he was doomed to the failure which duly resulted. For the rest of his life, like Baldwin, he maintained a detestation of Lloyd George.

Harold Wilson, in his *A Prime Minister on Prime Ministers*, has written of him:

He was one of the greatest municipal administrators and innovators in the history of local government – a record which was to be reflected in his years as Minister of Health under Baldwin. In Baldwin's cabinet of 1924–29, he was to carry through the most significant reforms in housing and local government seen in this century, at any rate until Aneurin Bevan.

One must never forget that he could have occupied the much higher position of Chancellor of the Exchequer during those years, but preferred a sphere where he felt he could make the most valuable contribution. Joseph Chamberlain's selection of the Colonial Office in 1895 provides an analogy.

When I worked in the Conservative research department Neville Chamberlain was much concerned with the tariff plans which were to be put into operation when he became Chancellor of the Exchequer. The other prong of his assault on the depression was an economy programme. I was secretary of the relevant committee. In the event, he must be given a large share of the credit for the recovery between 1931 and 1937. The conversion of War Loan from 5 per cent to a 3½ per cent basis was a triumph. Interest rates were kept amazingly low by present-day standards. The persistent unemployment of those years has seemed appalling until matched by similar figures in recent times. To many of us it seems appalling still, as does the present level. And there can be no comparison between the physical sufferings of those years and the years since the establishment of the welfare state.

Nevertheless, by any contemporary standard, Neville Chamberlain presided over an immense improvement in the national picture between 1931 and 1937; the average standard of life rose steadily.

A. J. P. Taylor, in his introduction to Montgomery Hyde's excellent short life of Neville Chamberlain, says this of him: 'Men either admired him greatly, or disliked him intensely. No Prime Minister had more devoted followers . . . yet there was always hostility to him. Labour people liked Baldwin and disliked Chamberlain, even though Baldwin had done little for the poor and Chamberlain a great deal.' Alan Taylor may have rather exaggerated the devotion of his followers. Nevertheless, there is no question that, at the time of Munich, the vast majority of Conservative MPs far preferred him to any alternative leader. That was probably still true when he fell from power in 1940. But I have no doubt from my talks with Lord Attlee that the Labour people could hardly bear him.

This was not very surprising when you read what has been written by his PPS, now Lord Home:

> He could not conceal his intellectual contempt for the Socialist Opposition in Parliament, and in particular for their pacifism, and in his speeches it showed. He would sting and sting again, and then strike for the kill. He was a skilled and merciless debater, and the Labour benches were routed over and over again. That was the basic reason why the Socialist leaders refused to come into a coalition under his leadership, even after he had declared war on behalf of the nation.

At this point it seems necessary to slip in another quotation from Lord Home:

> I must not give you the impression that Neville Chamberlain was an unattractive personality. He was a good naturalist – a really knowledge-able observer of birds, butterflies and animals. He liked fishing and shooting, and was skilled at them. He was fond too of music. None of this, however, was seen by the public, and his talents and attractions were kept for only a few intimate friends. That was his deliberate choice.

Which brings us to his foreign policy. Baldwin never had a foreign policy, that anyone could discover. Chamberlain pursued a distinc-tive foreign policy which has come to be known as appeasement. It was based on the hope of reaching a friendly understanding with Nazi Germany and Fascist Italy. He was convinced that such a policy was the only hope of averting a second world war. To the end of his life, he was satisfied that the attempt had been well worth while, and at the very worst had involved us in a war in which world opinion was solidly behind us.

Nowadays, when Chamberlain's policy of appeasement is attacked or defended one is usually thinking of his dealings with Hitler. In fact when Eden resigned as Foreign Secretary in February 1938 it was because of Chamberlain's attempt to establish friendly relations with Mussolini, to no small extent behind Eden's back. I have thought before now that when a member of a Prime Minister's government resigns he is more apt to be relieved than sorry. I should guess that this applied to the four resignations from Harold Wilson's Cabinet, including mine. Chamberlain in fact behaved in a way that left Eden no honourable course but resignation. This is not to say that the issue involved was primarily personal. Chamberlain stood for a policy of appeasement. Eden was utterly opposed to it. It was a genuine clash of principles.

The charges brought against Chamberlain's foreign policy can be placed under several broad headings, with considerable overlapping.

(1) the whole idea of appeasing the dictators was a grave error.
(2) Chamberlain continued with it when it was obviously leading to
disaster; partly due to his obstinate nature, partly due to his being
taken in by Hitler. (3) He failed to push on with rearmament at
anything like the speed required by the desperate situation of the
country. Two other more particular indictments are levelled at him:
that he betrayed Czechoslovakia at Munich, and that he failed to
conclude a defensive alliance with France and Russia.

I will not take these charges one by one, but will try to cover them
in what follows. Chamberlain's foreign policy has been endlessly
dissected, unfavourably for the most part. The authorized life by
Keith Feiling and the first volume of Churchill's war memoirs set the
scene. Two more Prime Ministers, Home and Wilson, have said their
say. When Chamberlain died Churchill delivered a characteristic
eulogy in the House of Commons. His deeper opinion is probably
that expressed with some restraint in *The Gathering Storm*:

> Neville Chamberlain . . . was alert, business-like, opinionated and
> self-confident in a very high degree. Unlike Baldwin, he conceived
> himself able to comprehend the whole field of Europe, and indeed the
> world. Instead of a vague but none the less deep-seated intuition, we now
> had a narrow, sharp-edged efficiency within the limits of the policy in
> which he believed. Both as Chancellor of the Exchequer, and as Prime
> Minister, he kept the tightest and most rigid control upon military
> expenditure.

At the time of Munich (September 1938) Churchill had been still
blunter:

> Five futile years of good intentions; five years of eager search for the line
> of least resistance; five years of uninterrupted defeat of British power;
> five years of neglecting the air defences. We have been reduced in these
> five years from a position so overwhelming and so unchallengeable. . . .

Home sums up succinctly. 'I am going to stick out my neck and say
that the British government was wrong about rearmament and right
about Munich.' On the first point I entirely agree with Lord Home.
As regards what is called 'Munich', one must divide the question into
the decision not to go to war at that moment and the general policy of
trying to sup with the devil. Today, I am more inclined than I was to
maintain that by the time of Munich we had got ourselves into a
position where we were totally unfitted to make war. On the wider
issue I have never altered my conviction that Chamberlain was
working along the wrong lines. At the time of Munich I was a Labour
councillor in Oxford. From a mixture of motives, perhaps, I paid

some unemployed men to dig trenches on Florence Park. Our output was not large. I remember being told in the City Engineer's office that the state of nerves precluded a high rate of productivity.

Home addresses himself carefully to the question as to why the Chamberlain government did not promote rearmament much more rapidly. He mentions various factors weighing with Chamberlain: (1) the likely reversal of the economic recovery; (2) the state of public opinion, not only here but throughout the Commonwealth; (3) the weakness of the French; (4) the menace of the Russians. But he acknowledges one 'real' mistake which Chamberlain made. 'He persuaded himself that where neither concessions, nor persuasion, nor power had changed Hitler's mind, his own reasonable approach could do so.' Here I have no doubt that Home is right, but he is not quite consistent.

In a later passage he asks whether Chamberlain was not culpably gullible. He answers this question in the negative. 'In any conversations that I had with him he showed no sign of having been duped. He had no illusions about Hitler's character. He looked upon him as boorish and crude and ruthless in his use of his power.'

I myself cannot forget what Chamberlain wrote to his sister after his first meeting with Hitler at Berchtesgaden in 1938. 'I had established a certain confidence which was my aim and on my side, in spite of the hardness and ruthlessness I thought I saw in his face, I got the impression that here was a man who could be relied upon, when he had given his word.' The awakening was painful indeed. My brother-in-law, Henry Lamb RA, was commissioned to paint Chamberlain after his Munich 'triumph'. Six months later, following Hitler's outrageous seizure of Prague, Henry noticed that Chamberlain was not wearing his usual overcoat. Asked about this, he replied that its associations were too bitter. It was the overcoat he had worn at Munich. Chamberlain was duped, and came to know that he had been duped, which made the end of his life all the more agonizing.

Chamberlain could not, or would not, believe until it was far too late that Hitler was a man devoid of morality in his own sense. His old friend Lord Swinton – maybe a little jaundiced by his own dismissal – wrote of him from inside knowledge and many years of intimate association:

He was the most pacific and honourable of men; the vast expenditure on rearming was something which shocked him; his mind could not reconcile itself to the justification of a massive arms programme. This, combined with a personal faith that he could handle the dictators and make them see reason, is the fairest judgement I can make to explain

Chamberlain, his motives, his ideals, his naivety, his courage and his disastrous obstinacy.

That word obstinacy should be examined more closely. No one who studies Neville Chamberlain's whole career can accuse him of undue self-centred ambition. No doubt he had an obsessive desire to do justice to the name of Chamberlain, but as a young man he was not, as we have seen, interested in politics and he did not seek to enter – and in fact did not enter – Parliament until he was close on fifty. He rejected the post of Chancellor of the Exchequer in 1924 in order to achieve social reforms in which he was passionately interested at the Ministry of Health. I can think of no parallel to this in my personal experience. His loyalty to Baldwin, though he was chafing repeatedly at what seemed to him the latter's indolence and ineptitude, was altogether exemplary.

But he had a profound conviction – we can call it a Chamberlainite conviction – that there were large areas of policy which he understood better than anyone else. This habit of mind grew on him. By the time he became Prime Minister in 1937 he assumed in his own mind a superior wisdom in regard to foreign affairs. And as a result he went grievously wrong. Once the true nature of Hitler and Hitlerism were revealed to him, his personal dilemma was insoluble. We can discuss today the question whether he should have resigned office not later than the outbreak of war, knowing himself to be so profound a man of peace that he was utterly unsuited for the role of war leader. However, for him to do so would have been to defy his whole nature, and the instinct which keeps a Prime Minister in office through so many adverse moments.

After the Norway disaster of 1940 it was inevitable that he should be removed from supreme office. He clung on to the last minute, and some would say beyond. But when he was supplanted he behaved with supreme dignity and loyalty as a member of Churchill's War Cabinet. Nothing became him better than these last few months as he approached his painful end. He died of cancer before the end of 1940.

It is unlikely that as the years pass there will be more approval of his policy of appeasement. Respect and sympathy for him as a man will grow.

Winston Churchill

The Warrior Prince

CHURCHILL
Rt Hon. Sir Winston (Leonard Spencer) (1874–1965)

M.P. (C) Oldham, 1900–4, (L) 1904–6;
(L) N.W. Manchester, 1906–8; (L) Dundee, 1908–18, (Co.L.) 1918–22;
(Const.) Epping Division of Essex, 1924–31, (C) 1931–45:
(C) Woodford, 1945–64.

Under-Secretary of State for the Colonies, 1906–8;
President, Board of Trade, 1908–10;
Home Secretary, 1910–11;
First Lord of the Admiralty, 1911–15;
Chancellor of Duchy of Lancaster, 1915;
Minister of Munitions, 1917;
Secretary of State for War and Air, January 1919–February 1921;
Air and the Colonies, February–April 1921;
and for the Colonies until October 1922;
Chancellor of the Exchequer, 1924–29;
First Lord of the Admiralty, 1939–40;
**Prime Minister, First Lord of the Treasury,
and Minister of Defence, 1940–45;**
Leader of the Opposition, 1945–51;
**Prime Minister and First Lord of the Treasury,
October 1951–April 1955;**
was also Minister of Defence, October 1951–January 1952.
K.G. 1953.

The Warrior Prince

HE HAD HAD TO WAIT a long time, till in fact he was sixty-five. Thirty-four years earlier he had said to Violet Bonham Carter, 'We are all worms but I do believe that I am a glow worm.' It had taken thirty years for his life to shine fully. Now he and Halifax were sitting with Chamberlain on the afternoon of 9 May 1940. The vote in the House of Commons on the previous day (though the Conservatives emerged with a nominal majority) had made certain beyond peradventure that Chamberlain could not remain Prime Minister. It was just as certain that the choice lay between Churchill and Halifax.

Two more contrasted representatives of aristocratic Britain could not be imagined. Halifax very tall, dignified, peace-loving, Christian, though not a Yorkshireman for nothing; Churchill stocky, militant alike in peace and war. Halifax intellectually distinguished in the best Oxford tradition, a Fellow of All Souls; Churchill a self-taught child of genius. There could be little doubt that Churchill was better suited to save the nation in its darkest moment. As against that, the majority of the Conservative Party, probably half the Labour Party and certainly the King preferred Halifax.

The outcome of the meeting was by no means assured at the beginning. Churchill has described his own performance in memorable words. 'I've had many important interviews in my public life and this was certainly the most important. Usually I talk a good deal but on this occasion I was silent. . . .' It was evident that Chamberlain preferred Halifax. 'As I remained silent,' writes Churchill, 'a very long pause ensued . . . then at length Halifax spoke. He said that his position as a peer out of the House of Commons would make it very difficult for him to discharge his duties as Prime Minister in a war like this.' That was, no doubt, a valid reason and it sufficed. It is known that Halifax was suffering from severe stomach-ache at the thought of assuming the war leadership, and that it immediately passed away when it became clear that the lot would fall upon Churchill.

The story of his appointment was not quite over yet. In the early hours of the next day the Germans invaded Holland and Belgium.

Chamberlain seemed to feel for a moment that it might be his duty to stay on. He was soon dissuaded. The Labour leaders, having sounded their conference, indicated that they were ready to serve under Churchill or Halifax; under anyone in fact except Chamberlain. So the King sent for Churchill, and at an extraordinary moment his life's ambition was realized. He felt with full justification that his whole life had been a preparation for this hour.

Winston Churchill is generally accepted as the greatest Englishman of the twentieth century. He is often referred to as the greatest Englishman of all time. He is frequently compared with the greatest world figures in history. When one bears in mind the difference this one man made to the survival of Britain and of Western freedom, these glories cannot be grudged him. Yet it all springs from five years, 1940–5, out of the ninety that he spent on the planet. Robert Rhodes James, a Conservative MP and a biographer of much repute, published a book about the life of Churchill up to 1939 under the title *Churchill, A Study in Failure*. If Churchill had died just before the election which he lost in 1945 his fame today would be as great and probably greater. His leadership of the Opposition and his premiership from 1951 to 1955, the latter marked by visibly declining powers, were by his own standards undistinguished. His warnings against the menace of Soviet communism could not have been so powerfully delivered by any other man. But the line he took was in fact the same as that being pursued by the Labour Government under Attlee.

Churchill is the only one of our eleven Prime Ministers to whom the word genius is applicable. It was recognized while he was still in his early thirties. Violet Asquith, daughter of the Prime Minister (later Violet Bonham Carter), meeting Winston for the first time at dinner in 1906, went to her father and told him that for the first time in her life she had seen genius. Asquith laughed and said, 'Well, Winston would certainly agree with you there, but I am not sure you would find many others of the same mind.' He added, however, 'Still, I know exactly what you mean; he is not only remarkable but unique.' Eighty years later we can readily accept that phrasing.

Churchill achieved early and maintained to the end a reputation for bad judgment. He never had a more devoted admirer or more valuable assistant than the present Sir John Colville. While Churchill was still First Lord of the Admiralty Colville, then his private secretary, wrote in his diary: 'Winston Churchill certainly gives one confidence and will I suspect be Prime Minister before the war is over. Nevertheless judging from his record of untrustworthiness and instability he may in that case lead us into the most dangerous paths.' He goes on to add, admittedly: 'He is the only man in the country who commands anything like universal respect and perhaps with age he has become less inclined to undertake rash adventures.' Despite those optimistic words Colville is treating it as a matter of accepted fact that Winston, then aged sixty-five, has to live down a record of untrustworthiness and instability.

Lord Moran, Churchill's medical adviser for so many years, whose book about him may or may not accord with medical ethics, had very close opportunities of judging. In his later years, when I saw a good deal of him, Moran repeated more than once the phrase, 'Winston had no judgment.' Attlee summed up the opinions of many when he remarked in old age, 'Winston half genius, half bloody fool.'

Winston Churchill's father, Lord Randolph Churchill, was Chancellor of the Exchequer by his middle thirties, and by his middle forties had died of a lingering disease. He was extraordinarily discouraging to Winston. Nor did his mother help him in his boyhood, though later she exerted herself tirelessly on his behalf. He was unsuccessful academically at Harrow, though he won a school prize for verse recitation. He was impelled to repair to a crammer for Sandhurst, which he managed to enter at the third attempt. By the time he was twenty-six he was in Parliament, already a national figure for his exploits and writings as a war journalist. By the time he was thirty-two he had switched from Conservative to Liberal, had become Under-Secretary for the Colonies and had written a massive biography of his father. The book was described by Lord Rosebery, himself a distinguished biographer if biased in Winston's favour, as one of the best half-dozen biographies in the language. In short, he was already a portent, if a very unpopular one in many quarters.

When he was thirty-six he was in the Cabinet as President of the Board of Trade (1908). He was Home Secretary from 1910 to 1911, and First Lord of the Admiralty from 1911 to 1915. By the outbreak of the war, he was one of the four most influential members of the Cabinet, the others being Asquith, Lloyd George and Grey. A year later the Gallipoli adventure led to his fall from real power and to public humiliation. 'I thought he would die of grief,' said his adoring but never uncritical wife Clementine. He set off for France, and commanded for several months (with considerable success) a battalion of the Royal Scots Fusiliers. He then returned to Parliament and was made Minister for Munitions by Lloyd George, on whose patronage much depended. His enormous energies made a big impression, but he was outside the circle of the war leaders.

A member of Lloyd George's coalition Cabinet (1918–22), he was one of the four British ministers who were primarily responsible for the Anglo-Irish Treaty of 1921, though he was the least significant.

His intense hostility to the new Soviet regime was long remembered there and elsewhere. In the 1922 General Election he lost, as he himself has written, as the same time his appendix, his ministerial post and his seat in Parliament.

But there was no keeping him down for long, or for that matter retaining him in the same party. He said later that you can rat but cannot re-rat. He himself, however, re-ratted most successfully. In 1924 he reappeared in Parliament as a Conservative and, to general amazement, as Chancellor of the Exchequer. Baldwin's reasons for the appointment have never been cleared up. The desire to prevent Winston from ganging up with Lloyd George seems to be an insufficient explanation.

Churchill was Chancellor of the Exchequer from 1924 to 1929; later in life he remarked, 'Everyone said I was the worst Chancellor of the Exchequer that ever was and now I am inclined to agree with them.' William Manchester in his vivid and well-researched account of Churchill's life up to 1932 considers that this self-criticism was going too far. The point is arguable. Manchester emphasizes Churchill's humanitarian role in the establishment of old age and widows' pensions. He insists that his attitude at the time of the General Strike was much less bellicose than was made to appear through his editorship of the *British Gazette*. There is no escaping, however, the magnitude of the error of returning to the gold standard at the old parity, a mistake which he bitterly regretted afterwards. He had much excuse at the time in an abundance of expert opinion. His determination to cut the defence estimates to the bone fits in well with the reasons that led to his father's resignation. It fits in not at all with his urgent demands soon afterwards that the national defences must be rapidly strengthened.

Soon after the fall of the Baldwin government he took a step which seemed for a long time to have ruined his career. He resigned from the Shadow Cabinet because of the Indian policy being pursued by Baldwin in particular. A prolonged struggle followed in which he revealed an attitude to India which today would find hardly any defenders. He took his stand on the simple conviction that the Indians would never be fit to govern themselves, and that in any case to give them independence would undermine the whole might of the British Empire. To quote one of his many glowing phrases: 'You will depress the British heartbeat all over the globe.'

I have suggested earlier that what followed was Baldwin's finest hour. His eloquence, if simpler, was during this period as potent as Churchill's own, and he was rooted in all that was most idealistic in British public opinion. Churchill was relying on prejudices acquired as a subaltern in India. It is a part of his life which his countless admirers pass over as rapidly as possible.

In the years that followed there was time before the war for Churchill to rise, fall and rise again. From the time when Hitler came to power in Germany in January 1933 Churchill began and continued a series of classic warnings which by 1939 had lifted his reputation to a higher point than ever previously. But there was one painful interruption in this process. At the time of the Abdication (1936) he chivalrously, if injudiciously, backed Edward VIII, and for the time being was once again lonely and discredited. However, the perils were too great, and his own convictions, based on much expert information, were so powerful that he became once again the name on every lip when the coming war was mentioned.

Churchill's attitude to Ireland fluctuated widely if predictably. At different times he said very different things about Irishmen and about Irish governments, but he did not leave the impression behind him of a friend of Ireland. Chamberlain, on the contrary, when he died was eulogized in Ireland more than elsewhere.

Churchill as a small boy had lived in the Viceregal Lodge, Dublin, when his grandfather was Lord-Lieutenant. Thirty years later he struck many hard blows on behalf of Home Rule. 'We shall put these grave matters to the proof,' was one of his best-remembered sayings. He had become the special *bête noire* of the Conservatives and the Ulster Unionists. Not only had he 'crossed the floor' and joined the Liberals; he was the son of the man who had arrogantly proclaimed, 'Ulster will fight and Ulster will be right.' Later he played a part in the group of British ministers who under Lloyd George negotiated the Anglo-Irish Treaty of 1921. 'What a team it was', I exclaimed in my account of the Treaty negotiations in my book *Peace by Ordeal* (1935) 'that could relegate Winston Churchill to fourth place.'

In the years that followed while I was writing my book Churchill's account of the proceedings held the field. It included a scathing indictment of the part played by De Valera. My own version has become a standard work, and must be deemed to have done something to redress the balance. But I have never ceased to admire the dramatic force of Churchill's narrative. In his final war volume, *The Aftermath*, his writing reached its highest point of eloquence.

Harold Wilson, in his illuminating, if uncritical, essay on Churchill in his book *A Prime Minister on Prime Ministers*, quotes a well-known remark attributed to Michael Collins: 'We would never have done anything without Winston.' The beautiful Lady Lavery, whose face later adorned the Irish coins and banknotes for many years, played a well-intentioned part during the Treaty negotiations (October to December 1921 in London). She undoubtedly did something to bring Churchill and Collins together socially. But for Churchill Collins was always the man 'whose hands had touched the springs of terrible deeds', and for Collins Churchill remained the aristocratic imperialist. Birkenhead and Collins became much more intimate. If Birkenhead had been a few years younger he would have enjoyed nothing more than a wrestling bout with Collins.

In the months following the Treaty Churchill, as Colonial Secretary, was the Minister directly responsible for making sure that the Treaty was enforced by Collins and his colleagues in Dublin. Churchill insisted on the suppression – by force if necessary – of armed resistance. Of Collins and the government in which he was the most potent factor, he asked the question, 'Will they die for the Treaty? Will they kill for it?' Collins was desperately anxious to avert the civil war which inexorably followed.

Lady Lavery described to me a painful visit which Collins paid to London. He had arrived by the night boat from Dublin, and had to return that evening. Civil war was very close. She took him down to see Churchill at Sir Philip Sassoon's house near London, but the butler informed them that Mr Churchill was painting and could not be disturbed. So it went on all day. Churchill found time for only a few words with Collins before the latter had to rush back.

Fairly or unfairly, De Valera could never overlook the pressure Churchill had exerted on the Griffith–Collins government at a time when it was just possible that civil war might have been averted. For many years Churchill on his side could not forgive De Valera for ruining (as it seemed to him) the glorious settlement embodied in the Treaty for which so many sacrifices had been made, both of political careers and of human life. We shall come across De Valera, the more Christian of the two, finding it harder to be forgiving. When I came to know Winston Churchill in the 1930s I could not discover whether he had read my book. His mind by that time was on other things. He murmured something about having so much to read. He gave me the impression that General Tudor, head of the paramilitary police, would have achieved victory over the Irish guerrillas if allowed to proceed. He vehemently objected to the Chamberlain–De Valera agreement of 1938 under which Britain renounced the use of facilities in the 'Irish Ports'.

I played no part myself in those negotiations. I was a Christ Church don at the time, teaching politics, including Anglo-Irish politics. Mr De Valera did, however, invite me to have coffee with him at the Piccadilly Hotel when the agreement with Chamberlain was concluded. With his usual courtesy he assured me that my account of the earlier negotiations had been of much assistance at this time. They had not failed on this occasion to put their demands on the table from the beginning. He might have added that, seventeen years older and now a world statesman, he had not made the mistake of himself staying in Dublin.

Later there was to be a rather unhappy aftermath. At the beginning of the Second World War I was having lunch in the Savoy Grill when Winston Churchill, First Lord of the Admiralty, and Leslie Hore-Belisha, Secretary of State for War, passed my table. Hore-Belisha stopped and asked me what I was doing. I told him that I had been seconded from my regiment, the Oxford and Buckinghamshire Light Infantry, to go over to Ireland for the Ministry of Information. It was a role as a double agent from which I extricated myself as soon as possible. Churchill pricked up his ears. 'I remember you', he said, 'as a friend of Randolph's, and unless I am mistaken of De Valera. You told Professor Lindemann that De Valera never expected to get back the Irish Ports [under the agreement of 1938]. You tell your friend De Valera that we have treated him with prodigal liberality, with unprecedented generosity, and what does he do? He sinks the *Courageous* [which had just been sunk by the Germans off the south-west coast of Ireland].' He stamped off, still breathing fire and slaughter.

Where Ireland was concerned, Churchill, no less than in the case of India, was living in the past. He simply could not get it into his head that Ireland, a self-governing Dominion, had a right to be neutral. He continued to regard the denial of the use of the Ports negotiated a year before with the British Government as odious. While First Lord of the Admiralty he was anxious that the Irish ports should be seized, by force if necessary. Mercifully, he was restrained. Roosevelt is supposed to have said of him: 'Winston has a hundred ideas a day, four of them good ones.' This was not a good one.

It may well seem to us now that when Chamberlain fell in May 1940 Churchill was the only conceivable choice. But, as explained above, the matter at the time was by no means so simple. Lord Home in his *Letters to a Grandson* has spelt out the reasons which led Churchill to be so widely suspected right up to the moment when he became Prime Minister.

A number of elderly Conservatives still blamed him for the spectacular failure of the Gallipoli expedition in the First World War. Even more had criticized his romantic support of the White Russian military campaign to overthrow the communist government. He was criticized by a different group for bringing us back to the gold standard at much too high a parity for the pound. The whole Labour Party and many others regarded his attitude to the independence of India as not only morally deplorable but politically fatuous. His gallant but hopelessly misjudged support for Edward VIII at the time of the Abdication added to the general conviction that there was something fatally wrong with his judgment.

Lord Moran used to tell me that Churchill had two supreme qualities: his will to prevail and his command of the English language. Harold Wilson has expanded the last point tellingly in his essay in *A Prime Minister on Prime Ministers*:

> Winston Churchill had through his power over words, but still more through his power over the hearts of men, that rare ability to call out from those who heard him the sense that they were a necessary part of something greater than themselves; the ability which runs like a golden thread through our national history to inspire a slumbering nation so that it can call up those inner reserves of effort and of character which have never failed us when our very survival has been at stake.

That is finely said. It could hardly be improved. However, Churchill was almost as eloquent when his warnings were neglected. Sometimes, as over India, he must seem to most of us now abysmally wrong. Sometimes, as he spelt out the Nazi menace, painfully right. But his stupendous words and his heroic potentialities made no deep appeal to his countrymen until the naked peril staring them in the face made him the one indispensable man.

To the Labour man in the street it hardly seemed credible that this extreme right-wing figure should head a national coalition, but the moment one heard his voice on the wireless one accepted it as the most natural thing in the world. My policy, he began, is to wage war. War to the uttermost. . . . Apart from outright pacifists, there can hardly have been a man or woman who did not feel inspired to give their all for the survival of the country from then on.

Churchill played down in after years his own incomparable contribution to victory: 'It was the nation and the race dwelling all round the globe that had the lion's heart. I had the luck to be called upon to give the roar.' At least one British historian, Liddell Hart, finds himself in substantial agreement with Churchill's modest self-assessment. Liddell Hart wrote: 'The British have always been less dependent than other people upon inspiring leadership. . . . It may be a necessity when they are weary, but not when they have had a slap in the face. It was Dunkirk that braced them in June 1940, more than any individual influence.' But here assuredly Liddell

Hart was wrong, though the *difference* Churchill made to Britain throughout those tumultuous years could never be measured.

Out of his many unforgettable speeches, there is room for a quotation from only one. It was the speech which he delivered to Parliament on 4 June 1940, when the Dunkirk evacuation was officially declared complete. The tremendous peroration echoed throughout the world:

> Even though large tracts of Europe and many old and famous States have fallen or may fall into the grip of the Gestapo and all the odious apparatus of Nazi rule, we shall not flag or fail. We shall go on to the end, we shall fight in France, we shall fight in the seas and oceans, we shall fight with growing confidence and growing strength in the air, we shall defend our Island whatever the cost may be, we shall fight on the beaches, we shall fight on the landing grounds, we shall fight in the fields and in the streets, we shall fight in the hills; we shall never surrender. . . .

As he sat down a few moments later he was heard by those next to him to murmur: 'We'll beat the b . . . . . . s over the head with broomsticks, it's all we've got.'

The entire public and millions overseas were each affected according to their own nature. That most sophisticated of women, Vita Sackville-West, wrote to her husband Harold Nicolson: 'Even repeated by the announcer it sent shivers (not of fear) down my spine. I think that one of the reasons why one is stirred by his Elizabethan phrases is that one feels the whole massive backing of power and resolve behind them, like a great fortress: they are never words for words' sake.' The overwhelming impact on the public was deliberate and sustained. There was a moment when Churchill felt compelled to ask the Chiefs of Staff for an appreciation of the prospects of victory or even survival. He elicited an opinion from which he drew the conclusion that everything would depend on our civilian morale. This he set out to strengthen and enhance in every conceivable fashion, and never wavered from that purpose.

I can remember personally paying great attention to his report that he had been assured by the Chiefs of Staff that we could fight on with 'good and reasonable chances' of victory. No doubt he was correctly representing their views as expressed; but a weaker, or less inspired, leader might well have obtained a very different appreciation.

Moving on two years from 1940, one comes across Lord Moran's example of his sublime 'gutfulness' at a moment when a lesser man would have been humiliated and cast down. Lord Moran found his heart going out to 'this unbeatable man'. President Roosevelt, his host for the third time, had just handed Churchill a telegram in silence. The telegram read: 'Tobruk has surrendered with 25,000 men taken prisoners.' At Singapore and now at Tobruk British armies had surrendered to an inferior number of enemy forces. Defeat is one thing, Churchill noted, disgrace is another. But in Lord Moran's account, 'with our military prestige at zero here he has dominated the discussion'. No anecdote could better epitomize his attitude at all times during the war years.

Whether he was a good, bad or indifferent strategist will always be disputed. The question can never be settled, if only because the merit of his decisions (and of course they were not his alone) will never be distinguished from the moral and psychological effect of his leadership. Controversies will go on raging about our first attempt to rescue Greece. About the loss of the *Prince of Wales* and *Repulse*. About the strategy that led up to the fall of Singapore. About the raid on Dieppe and many other episodes. Even assuming that in the cases mentioned serious mistakes were made, and that Churchill played a large part in making them, we cannot begin to stack them up against the vast number of decisions which have not aroused criticism. We must recognize, moreover, that once Russia and America were our allies we were in no position to insist on having our way in crucial directions. Nevertheless, in the middle of 1940 when Churchill became Prime Minister it seemed most unlikely to a dispassionate observer such as the American Ambassador Joe Kennedy that Britain would pull through, and no words could ever do justice to the extent of his war achievement.

Winston Churchill occupied a large place in my thoughts for some years before I met him, and long before he became a world hero. I am ashamed, however, to think of the laugh I raised at a meeting of the Eton political society in 1923, when some eminent visitor was assessing the future prospects of various leaders. 'Do you think', I asked, 'that Mr Winston Churchill [out of Parliament at the time, and not yet restored to the Conservative fold] has any future?' The whole idea seemed ridiculous to the visitor and his Etonian audience. None of us boys (I cannot speak for the masters) would have read his brilliant life of his father. None of us would have recalled his radical achievements, especially at the Home Office in the pre-1914 Asquith Cabinet. It is doubtful how many of us would have been aware that he had the Fleet ready in 1914. We knew that twice at least he had come unstuck since that time, and now was very much in the wilderness.

But when I read the four volumes of his history of the First World War I passed at once under his spell. If I had been asked, about 1930, who were my favourite contemporary prose writers I should have picked out two disparate authors, Winston Churchill and W. B. Yeats (for his autobiographies). Out of the blue I was invited to become secretary of the India Defence League, the organization set up to hold back the march of India to independence. Churchill was present when I attended their committee. Though not the chairman he was the ruling spirit. He sat there scowling, or at any rate frowning. I was flattered by the offer, but had no intention of accepting it. When I met my mother afterwards she made one of her few political comments. 'You would never have been able to look me in the face if you had accepted a position under Winston Churchill.'

My father, I should explain, had been killed at Gallipoli, leading his brigade in person. Some years later when I met Churchill's most faithful disciple, Brendan Bracken, at Cliveden, the Astors' house, he recited impromptu what Churchill had written in his *World Crisis*. 'On that battlefield of fog and flame fell Brigadier General The Earl of Longford . . . and other Paladins.' My mother would have been familiar with those words. As the widow of a professional soldier she would have ordinarily accepted his death with resignation. But nothing could reconcile my mother and numerous other Gallipoli widows to the man they held responsible for the gratuitous slaughter. Historically unfair, no doubt. Nevertheless, that sincere attitude affected Churchill's public standing for many years.

By this time (1930) I had become a close friend of the Birkenhead family. I had come to look on their country house, Charlton, as my second home. Churchill and Birkenhead had long been intimate friends across the party division. I was brought, so to speak, to the edge of the Churchill circle. Randolph Churchill, somewhat younger than Freddy, later the second Lord Birkenhead, had been brought up in a close, if rather ambivalent, relationship with him.

While Randolph was still at Eton I, still at Oxford, had been called on to take the headmaster's division in modern subjects for a fortnight. Playing for time, I had asked each member of the form to select his favourite piece from the *Oxford Book of English Prose*. That took up one period. Another was occupied in the delivery of the chosen passages, a third in carrying out a mock-election regarding the merits of the various performers. A golden-haired youth had chosen the end of Macaulay's essay on Warren Hastings, and declaimed it like a Prime Minister of the future. However, when the poll was taken he received no votes at all. I asked why. I was told, 'Oh, that's Randolph Churchill. He's far too bumptious.'

When he arrived at Oxford I became much attached to him. My only public appearance at his side did not prove helpful. In the spring of 1933 the Oxford Union passed the notorious resolution declining to fight for King and Country. Winston Churchill has remarked that 'These foolish boys were soon to conquer or fall gloriously and prove themselves the finest generation ever bred in Britain.' Randolph, by this time an undergraduate, conceived it his patriotic duty to get the resolution expunged. His father no doubt approved. I could not resist his appeal to join him. Randolph, whatever his failings, never lacked courage. On this occasion he met with a very ugly reception. Stink-bombs rained down on us from the gallery. The cry went up, 'To the Cherwell with both of them!' We were lucky to escape intact. It remained a bond between us.

My feeling that Churchill, though a superlative writer, was a man without much political future was slightly but not fundamentally altered when Randolph Churchill took me down to lunch with his father at Chartwell in autumn 1935. He came in to lunch from building a wall and no doubt working out new phrases for his life of Marlborough. At first he was somewhat grumpy, but as the wine flowed his eloquence expanded and for three hours the small company were treated to an harangue which I had never heard equalled.

Somewhere around four o'clock, whiskies and sodas were called for, and not long afterwards I was emboldened to ask him, 'If the Germans are already as strong as you say, what could we do if they landed here?' He replied, 'That should not prove an insoluble conundrum. We are here five able-bodied men.' Our backs began to straighten, our shoulders squared. 'The armoury at our disposal is not perhaps very modern, but none of us would be without a weapon. We should sally forth. I should venture to assume the responsibilities of command. If the worst came to the worst, we should sell our lives dearly. Whatever the outcome we should, I feel confident, render a good account of ourselves.'

And I feel confident that at that moment we should have done so, with the whiskies and sodas inside us, with our eyes shining and every nerve aflame.

Yet it never crossed my mind that this great man in exile, this brooding genius from the past, would ever again occupy one of the supreme positions, let alone the supreme position in British politics.

Winston Churchill's house was about four miles from that of Elizabeth's mother. We went to tea there more than once. I cannot recall much prolonged political conversation. Tea was not a Churchillian meal. I did, however, draw closer to Churchill in spirit through my close friendship with Professor Lindemann, later Lord Cherwell, my Christ Church colleague and frequent golf companion.

He was Churchill's scientific adviser then and throughout the war, and in some respects his most intimate friend. 'Prof' was equally close to the Birkenhead and Churchill families, and frequently motored me over to the Birkenheads' house at Charlton.

Hardly a day passed without the Prof telling me the latest news about Churchill's desperate struggle to awaken the Government to the need for rapid rearmament; and in particular to the urgent requirements of air defence. By 1936 I was becoming an active member of the Labour Party. From certain points of view, Churchill and the Prof were appalling reactionaries, but I became utterly convinced of the rightness of their attitude to rearmament.

During the Oxford by-election which followed the Munich agreement (autumn 1938) Randolph appeared in Oxford to offer private support for the independent progressive, the Master of Balliol, against the official Conservative, the future Lord Hailsham. While he was with us his father telephoned to send personal good wishes. Soon afterwards I became Labour candidate for Oxford. In retrospect, our Labour Party line at that time seems to make little sense. We were still persuading ourselves that support for collective security would provide adequate defence without rapid rearmament. So it would have done a few years earlier, but certainly not by 1939. When a measure of conscription was introduced in spring 1939 the Labour Party voted against it, which Attlee and other leaders later admitted was a mistake. My own pathetic demonstration was to join the Territorials, an adventure more glorious in the intention than in the result.

I remember very well a visit that Winston paid to the Oxford Union not long before the war, the hall having been hired by the Conservative Association. Bearing in mind that in this same hall six years earlier the 'King and Country' resolution had been carried and, to the extreme discomfiture of Randolph, been confirmed, he was ecstatically happy at the transformation in the attitude of young Oxford. He was loudly applauded by members of all parties. Recalling earlier experiences, he remarked endearingly, 'I have not changed but you have trained on.' He could have led us anywhere that night.

In the war years I had no contact with him after the encounter recalled before in the Savoy Grill. I saw quite a lot, however, during the war of three of his staunchest henchmen, Randolph, Professor Lindemann and Brendan Bracken. Randolph at one point asked me to become his Assistant Military Spokesman in Cairo. The Prof jealously guarded the PM's interest in the Oxford common-rooms. Woe betide the incautious public servant who expressed any criticism. A cousin of Elizabeth's, the brilliant Director of Naval Intelligence Admiral Godfrey, (the 'M' of Ian Fleming stories) soon found himself in India trying to cope with a mutiny after some frank criticisms in the Christ Church senior common-room.

My connection with Brendan Bracken, Minister of Information, became quite close at the end of 1942. I was Beveridge's personal assistant. At the time the report was published the very wind of Beveridge's name had swept to the ends of the earth. At that time it was better known than that of any Englishman other than Churchill, and for a few weeks more constantly spoken than Churchill's own. The whole attitude, however, of Churchill to Beveridge and his report was indifferent to hostile. Here was someone anxious to behave towards him with loyalty and deference. But neither then, when his preoccupations were admittedly colossal, nor more remarkably when he came to write his war memoirs, did he show towards Beveridge a trace of his habitual and glorious magnanimity.

At the time Beveridge was undoubtedly pained. He was welcomed at Buckingham Palace, but Churchill declined a respectful suggestion that Beveridge should come to see him. He sent him, admittedly, a handsome wedding present – four volumes of *Marlborough* – and Mrs Churchill attended Beveridge's wedding. So did Brendan Bracken, who made a delightful speech and gracefully covered up the absence of the Prime Minister. But Beveridge was never employed by the Coalition Government in the remaining two and a half years of war.

Harold Wilson is fully entitled to point with admiration to Churchill's speeches in favour of social reform when he was a young Minister in Asquith's government. I would add my personal tribute to his boldness as Home Secretary, above all to the unique amnesty which he granted to a large number of prisoners. But taking the last half-century of his life, he could not be described as a social reformer.

In the post-war years, I continued to be friends with Randolph. His compelling charm – though he had long since lost the beauty of his youth – more than compensated for his intermittent offensiveness. He had a habit of ringing up his friends after midnight. Once he rang me up at 2 a.m. to ask me to come down to his house at East Bergholt to participate in a television programme. I showed myself willing, but in a bemused way began to discuss the logistics. He became impatient and broke off with the words, 'You're nothing but a bloody socialist anyway.' One put up with such things from Randolph as from no one else except an even closer friend, Evelyn Waugh.

After the war I saw Churchill fairly often. In summer 1947 I had recently become Minister for Germany, and was propounding the ideas of Christian friendship towards that stricken country. They were by no means in harmony with those agreed between the two victorious Powers at Potsdam, and still supported officially by the Labour Government and the Conservative opposition. I told the nearly starving children of the Ruhr that they were absolutely right to be proud of being Germans, which did not go down at all well with my superiors. It was to lead to my being transferred elsewhere. At the Buckingham Palace garden party, Churchill, then Leader of the Opposition, spotted me from afar and lumbered towards me. I would never have ventured to approach him. 'I am glad', he spelt out slowly, 'that there is one mind suffering for the miseries of Germany.' Seeking to improve the phrase, he amplified it: 'One English mind suffering for the miseries of Germany.' Irishman though I am, I have never appreciated a compliment quite so much.

He had already made his Fulton speech denouncing the Iron Curtain. He was desperately worried about the Soviet menace. He had said when Bevin was appointed Foreign Secretary in 1945, 'I am glad that my friend Ernest Bevin is to be Foreign Secretary. He'll sprawl all over the map of Europe but at least he's against the Communists.' However, there was an extraordinary reluctance among the political leaders of that time to recognize that, Christian ethics apart, it was impossible to hold down the Germans with one hand, and to hold back the Russians with the other. I never doubted from that brief moment together at the garden party in 1947 that Churchill would do all in his power to bring back Germany on an equal footing as a partner in the Western Alliance.

Six years later in 1953, as chairman of the Anglo-German Association, I was invited to a grand dinner at No. 10 Downing Street which Churchill was giving for Dr Adenauer, then German Chancellor. While I was still Minister for Germany in 1948 I had helped to facilitate the visit of Adenauer to the Hague Conference. It represented an important step in the building up of the European movement whose inspiration owed so much to Churchill. Adenauer told me afterwards that he had not pressed himself on Churchill. He admired him enormously, but he was understood to have said that Germans are either at your feet or at your throat, and this, said Adenauer, 'was the hour of my country's humiliation'. Churchill characteristically had overwhelmed him with courteous attention.

On this 1953 occasion in Downing Street all the right things were said, and said with evident sincerity, but I remember most easily an exchange between Churchill and Lord Montgomery. The latter was standing with me on the edge of the circle of guests when Churchill joined us. 'Don't you think, Prime Minister,' said Monty, pointing to me, 'that his hair wants cutting?' My hair grows freely, though not in the right places. Monty's role was that of a military gentleman teasing an absent-minded professor. Churchill as always delivered his words slowly and carefully: 'Your head, my dear Field Marshall,' said he, 'requires compression under a military cap. He needs his for speaking in the House of Lords.'

Churchill to the end of his life found it necessary to prepare his speeches carefully in advance. And yet in the course of a day he probably coined impromptu a dozen phrases to compare with the one just quoted. As always, one could not separate the words from the human being.

He was kind to me on a number of social occasions. His son-in-law Christopher Soames and his daughter Mary gave Elizabeth and me intense pleasure by inviting us to meet him and Lady Churchill on more than one occasion at their house. Mary used to refer to her father as 'Christopher's university'. If that is so, it has stood him in good stead ever since. He does not imitate his father-in-law, and yet when he addresses the House on international affairs I can almost hear the grand old man speaking.

On one occasion Randolph asked us to a small birthday dinner he was giving his father. Winston was very benign towards me, as a young Labour politician. I represented, he said, the same slice of the country as he had during his Liberal years. I came away with the feeling that he had not much affection for any political party, Liberal, Tory or what you will. But he had a warm feeling for the Labour leaders who had stood by him so loyally during the war coalition. Churchill was concerned only with the past, present and future of Britain. There was no intrinsic change in that respect since my 1935 visit to Chartwell.

Socially, the encounter I remember best occurred at The Other Club, the highly select dining club of which he was the co-founder and presiding genius. This was in the early sixties, by which time his powers had much declined. I was a new member. An attempt was always made to represent all parties, but for one reason or another not many Labour politicians were members. The other new member was Onassis, on whose yacht Churchill had been staying. My first impression was that Churchill knew Onassis well enough but had no idea of my identity. This impression persisted throughout dinner, at which I sat opposite him. Towards the end he suddenly raised his champagne glass and looked across at me. He shot me the sweetest of smiles, and then relapsed into obliviousness.

When he became Prime Minister he made an attempt to secure

Irish co-operation in the war, but a shadowy suggestion in the direction of Irish unity was too little and too late. When America entered the war he sent De Valera a euphoric telegram in the middle of the night, but he was never in a position to promise the consent of the Ulstermen. So nothing occurred. De Valera indicated to me more than once during the war that if it had been postponed a few years an agreement to secure the unity of Ireland might indeed have been reached with Chamberlain. He implied that in that case Ireland might well have been fighting alongside the Allies, where their sympathies lay. As it was, there was no such possibility. When Hitler died on 30 April 1945, De Valera performed the diplomatic courtesy of calling on the German Ambassador in Dublin. Churchill, like many others in Britain, reacted furiously. He sank well below his normal standard in denouncing De Valera for the whole policy he had pursued throughout the war. Churchill boasted of the fact that Britain had not obtained by force the facilities denied them.

I was in Dublin when De Valera replied, with all Ireland hanging on his words. Calm and dignified, he was at his best. Soon after the war, I introduced Randolph Churchill to him. He took pleasure in informing Dev that his father considered that Dev had had the better of the exchanges. He himself (Winston) had made a false move in patting himself on the back for his restraint. Dev told me about that time that if he had been an Englishman he would have voted for Churchill in the General Election: I should like to think that he told that to Randolph, but I doubt whether he would have thought it appropriate.

As time went on, Churchill's attitude to De Valera mellowed. De Valera (whose biography I came to write) told me that at meetings of the Council of Europe Churchill began to show him special attention. A little hard of hearing by now, he would come over and sit below the rostrum when De Valera was speaking, cupping his ear in his hand. There came a moment when Churchill, as Prime Minister, entertained De Valera to lunch at 10 Downing Street with the utmost cordiality. One of Churchill's secretaries told me that Churchill got quite excited beforehand. By that time De Valera, so long a bogeyman, had become a respectable part of history.

De Valera never quite got used to Churchill's play-acting, which amused but baffled him. He refrained from coming over to Churchill's funeral, Ireland being represented by her Minister of External Affairs. De Valera as a devout Christian would have felt a strong obligation to forgiveness. Nevertheless in his eyes it was impossible to dissociate Churchill from the origins of the Irish Civil

War. He would have been betraying his old comrades if he had attended the funeral.

Except where his prejudices were aroused, Churchill had a profound feeling for international relationships. He gave a tremendous fillip to the European movement in the years after the war. When he returned to office as Prime Minister he was seventy-six. An anticlimax followed in his attitude to Europe. His handling of Anglo-American relations was a sublime feat, second only to the moral leadership he supplied to the British people. He had the advantage, no doubt, of an American mother, but that supplied him with no more than a starting-point. From the beginning of the war, President Roosevelt was writing the first of his wartime letters to Churchill – the first of eight hundred – while Churchill was to contribute over nine hundred. With all Roosevelt's prestige, goodwill and political astuteness, he could not bring the United States into the war before they were attacked by Japan. However, by that time Britain had received an enormous volume of material help and the way had been prepared for the full-blooded co-operation that followed.

Churchill calls the last volume of his war history *Triumph and Tragedy*. As a dramatic historian he cannot resist describing the failure of the democracies as analogous to their failure after the war of 1914–18. His interpretation is hard to follow. The villain of this last volume is naturally Soviet Russia, more particularly Stalin, but the folly on the face of it must be attributed to the United States, primarily Roosevelt. Churchill does not like to say this too clearly for obvious reasons, neither does he accept any measure of blame himself. He indicates the possibility that, if he had survived the General Election, better terms could have been obtained at the Potsdam Conference. But who believes that today?

Let us join in blaming Stalin to our heart's content, and also if we must the dying Roosevelt. However, in this book we are discussing British Prime Ministers and comparing the limitations under which each of them has operated. Neville Chamberlain's assumptions about Hitler were denounced by Churchill, and have been treated by historians as those of an idiot. But was Churchill all that much wiser than his unhappy predecessors? Churchill said at Yalta, as he dined with Stalin, 'It is no exaggeration or compliment of a florid kind when I say that we regard Marshal Stalin's life as most precious to the hopes and hearts of all of us.' Neville Chamberlain never said anything as foolish as that about Hitler. In fairness, though, part of Churchill's answer to such a charge must at least be given: 'What would have happened if we had quarrelled with Russia while the Germans still had two or three hundred divisions on the fighting front? Our hopeful assumptions were soon to be falsified. Still, they were the only ones possible at the time.'

Churchill the great phrase-maker cannot be encapsulated in a phrase, though the attempt has been made on numerous occasions. Perhaps Sir Isaiah Berlin went closest to the heart of the matter when he said of him, 'Churchill created a heroic mood.' Created and sustained it through five traumatic, often agonizing years. He had the courage of a hero, the language of an artist; above all he shared during those years the deepest feelings of the people in the innermost core of his own being. He strengthened those convictions immeasurably by giving them sublime expression.

Clement Attlee

The Servant of the People

ATTLEE
Rt Hon. Sir Clement Richard
(1883–1967)

M.P. (Lab.) Limehouse Division of Stepney, November 1922–February 1950;
West Walthamstow, 1950–5.

Parliamentary Private Secretary to the Leader of the Opposition
(Rt. Hon. J. Ramsay MacDonald), 1922–4;
Under-Secretary of State for War, 1924;
Chancellor of the Duchy of Lancaster, 1930–1;
Postmaster-General, 1931;
Member of the Indian Statutory Commission, 1927;
Deputy Leader of the Labour Party in the House of Commons, 1931–5;
Leader of the Opposition, 1935–40;
Lord Privy Seal, 1940–2;
Secretary of State for Dominion Affairs, 1942–3;
Lord President of the Council, 1943–5;
Deputy Prime Minister, 1942–5;
Prime Minister and First Lord of the Treasury, 1945–51;
Minister of Defence, 1945–6;
Leader of the Opposition, 1951–5.

Created 1st Earl Attlee, 1955;
K.G. 1956.

The Servant of the People

CLEMENT ATTLEE LOOMS LARGER and larger as a statesman of the first order, and a very remarkable and entertaining personality. The contributors to a centenary volume, following up the splendid biography by Kenneth Harris, pay ample tribute to the strength of his moral convictions. But just as enjoyable are the highly idiosyncratic anecdotes.

Roy Jenkins has this to say of him:

> His incisiveness expressed itself in laconicism. For nearly the first sixty years of his life this probably stemmed more from shyness and lack of fluency than from choice. But as his reputation grew so what would previously be regarded as jejuneness came to be seen as the epitome of pith, towards the end as almost a national institution. Very sensibly he somewhat cultivated this, and enjoyed being just a little of a caricature of himself.

The most famous of all his laconic replies – 'They call me laconic,' he used to say to me with some satisfaction – is that to Harold Laski, who as chairman of the Labour Party took it on himself to hector Attlee, the new Prime Minister. 'A period of silence on your part', Attlee is now said to have replied, 'will be advantageous.' I prefer to think of him as having said 'would be welcome', which is after all two syllables shorter.

The story is often told of his saying to a Minister who asked why he was being dismissed, 'No good.' (One wonders where this story started.) I was not aware before of a wittier piece of dialogue recorded by Woodrow Wyatt. Attlee sent for a Labour MP and said that his betrayal of the confidences of a royal person 'was not the behaviour of a gentleman'. 'I don't', said the Labour MP, 'quite know what you mean.' 'Exactly,' retorted Attlee. I cannot quite believe that he delivered a still sharper retort attributed to him by Lord Home and others. A visitor who had outstayed his welcome paused at the door and asked, 'Is there anything more I can do for you, Prime Minister?' 'Yes,' replied Attlee without looking up, 'go.'

The trouble about these and many other similar anecdotes founded at least on truth is that they give an impression of Attlee as a bad-tempered man. They fail altogether to bring out his consistent kindness. Christopher (now Lord) Mayhew, dear to Attlee as an Old Haileyburian but not only for that reason, supplies a good corrective:

> Unlike most successful political leaders, Clement Attlee was entirely unspoilt by fame and power. I remember a rather large and formal dinner he gave at Chequers when he was Prime Minister – black ties, long dresses, and several famous faces. After assembling in the hall, we were ushered into the dining-room where it became apparent, as we sat down, that someone was missing. Told that this was a school-friend of his daughter, Felicity, who was late, Clem Attlee told us to refold our napkins and hurry back to the hall. There we all waited until the little girl came downstairs, unsuspecting, and joined us. We then went into dinner again as though for the first time.

No doubt Attlee was much more soft-hearted at home than in public controversy, but he was basically not only a modest but a benevolent man.

He is not usually thought of as a poet, but the *Attlee Memorial Volume* does well to include some of his verses to which I at least would not deny the title of poetry. His work in the East End before the war stirred him profoundly. I have only space for one example:

LONDON RIVER

O, London river rolling to the sea
Your weight of weary waters sad and brown
Upon your dusky bosom bearing down
Light skiff and heavy laden argosy
Devious and slow your journey seems to be.
Threading the close packed reaches of the town
By squalid tenements of ill renown,

Where thousands dwell in want and misery.
So in our age of poverty and grime
A sluggish winding stream our progress proves
So short the forward step, so weak our feet.
Yet list we to the watchers of the time,
Who, weighing well advancement and retreat,
Cry out with Galileo 'Yet it moves'.

Attlee was born in 1883. His father was a prominent solicitor, at one time president of the Law Society. Clem was educated at Haileybury and University College, Oxford, making little mark in either establishment. At school he was too small and light to be good at games, though he excelled in the OTC, a point of some significance later. At Oxford he obtained a half-blue for billiards, benefiting from many happy hours spent earlier on a billiard table. Intellectually he was a late developer. As his Oxford 'schools' approached, his tutors began to hold out the possibility of a First. In fact he obtained a Second, but the ability was there for those who could look beyond his unobtrusive appearance. He took his degree in 1904. He entered legal chambers, but in 1905 became involved in the Haileybury boys' club in Stepney. In 1907 he became its resident manager. He also served for a time as secretary of the Toynbee Hall Settlement, an institution to which he showed himself indefatigably loyal in the years of his greatness.

His experience in the East End of London converted him to socialism. He joined the Fabian Society in 1907, but found it too middle-class in attitude. By 1908 he was a member of the Stepney branch of the Independent Labour Party, and for a time became its secretary.

Kenneth Harris sums up well the life he led and the impression he made during those years. 'He was always the servant. He never set the pace himself, never emerged as a natural leader who by oratory or agitation caused other men to follow.' 'I had no idea', said Attlee, 'of anything more than working as a member of the rank and file, and perhaps getting on to a local council.' I can think of no other Prime Minister who could have said that kind of thing and be believed. The fact that he did more and talked less than any other socialist in Stepney was widely observed.

When war broke out (1914), Attlee and his dearly loved brother Tom — absorbed like himself in social work — followed different paths, though their mutual affection never wavered. Tom became a pacifist, and later went for a while to prison. Attlee from Haileybury days had always admired the military virtues and enjoyed the military way of life. The Haileybury boys' club was run on the lines of a cadet corps. For many years after the First World War, the title of Major Attlee would seem appropriate. In any case his form of patriotism was always direct and uncomplicated.

His record in the First World War was typical of the man, reminiscent indeed of his social work in the East End. He served in the South Lancashire Regiment and in the Tank Corps. At Gallipoli he commanded part of the rearguard. He was wounded in Mesopotamia and again in France. He emerged with the rank of major, but was otherwise unrecognized except by those who had served with him. More than once it was expected that he would at least be mentioned in despatches, but all through his early life, deliberately or otherwise, he did good by stealth. It was only much later that he 'blushed to find it fame'. Churchill did honour more than once to Major Attlee, who had been through some of the heaviest fighting.

The war was not long over when Attlee returned to the East End and resumed a rather humble position at the same time at the London School of Economics. He became Mayor of Stepney, and by 1922 he was elected as a Labour MP for Limehouse. He was Under-Secretary for War in Ramsay MacDonald's first government, 1923–4; Labour member of the Simon Commission to India, an appointment which undoubtedly provided him with the self-confidence required for his tremendous Indian initiative twenty years later; in MacDonald's second government Chancellor of the Duchy of Lancaster without portfolio and Postmaster-General outside the Cabinet. He is barely noticed by Beatrice Webb in her diaries for these years, which dwell extensively on other Labour personalities.

After the Labour Party débâcle in 1931 he found himself deputy leader to George Lansbury, his more prominent contemporaries having fallen by the wayside. Not quite yet a member of the Labour Party, I attended as a visitor the historic conference at Brighton, when the issue was fought out before the world as to whether Mussolini's aggression against Abyssinia should in the last resort be resisted by force. When I listen to or participate in nuclear debates today the old echoes are unfailingly aroused. The Christian arguments for or against war in any shape or form change little over the years. I can still hear Lansbury crying, 'As Christ said in the Garden, those who take the sword will perish by the sword. There I have taken my stand and there, if necessary, I will die.' The thousands of delegates rose to him, and for the moment it seemed that he would prevail. But Ernie Bevin came along, in his massive flat-footed way, confident that in the last resort he had on his side the block vote of the unions. 'I'm not going to 'ave George Lansbury 'awking his conscience all round Europe,' he declared with a conviction as overpowering as Lansbury's own. Lansbury was swept into the discard, and his own resignation followed soon after. Major Attlee, as he was still called, appropriately took his place.

As his allegedly more glamorous rivals made their way back to Parliament he was challenged for the leadership of the Labour Party, but he was as tenacious, once elected, as he had been unselfseeking in pursuing office. His reign as Leader of the Labour Party was to last for twenty years, and to end only when in his early seventies he decided to call it a day.

From 1935 to 1940, he proved an efficient Leader of the Opposition. He held the party together, and when called on by Churchill to join a coalition he could deliver the goods. From 1940 to 1945 he was a self-effacing deputy leader who made sure that the Labour Party played a full part in the war effort and at the same time never forgot for a moment the socialist aspirations of his half of England. Sir John Rodgers has told a story of which one likes to be reminded. Rodgers, a Conservative admirer of Attlee, had for once said something derogatory about him. He had referred to 'silly old Attlee'.

> Winston stopped me and said, 'What did you say?' I repeated this, thinking he hadn't heard me. He interrupted me again and said: 'Mr Attlee is Prime Minister of England. Mr Attlee was Deputy Prime Minister during the war, and played a great part in winning the war. Mr Attlee is a great patriot. Don't you dare call him 'silly old Attlee' at Chartwell or you won't be invited again.'

By the time the Second World War came, I, as an Oxford don, Labour councillor and candidate for Oxford, had come to know him fairly well. He visited Oxford quite often. When Anthony Eden resigned in February 1938 there was terrific excitement in the Labour Party. Could this be the beginning of the end of 'Chamberlainism'? The town hall was packed. I was in the chair. The vociferous enthusiasm seemed to suit Attlee. It meant that he did not have to generate emotion himself. He had no difficulty in sharing it, though his language was as restrained as ever. After the meeting we carried him in triumph up the High Street and then back to the station. That he most definitely did not enjoy. But he looked back on the occasion in after-years with satisfaction.

One wartime episode does not show Attlee at his most genial, but is worth relating. The Beveridge Report on Social Insurance – but its implications were far wider – came out at the end of 1942. I had been working for the previous two years as Beveridge's personal assistant. The report took the world by storm. Early in 1943, Beveridge was still enormously admired. He was politically unattached, but the Labour Party were almost unanimous in claiming his ideas as in conformity with theirs, though he stopped a long way short of socialism. It would have been a great coup for the Labour Party if he had joined them, and on the face of it, this was a reasonable proposition.

Attlee's PPS at the time was Arthur Jenkins, father of Roy – an ex-miner, though he looked more like a poet. Attlee, as we know, had a *penchant* alike for miners and poetry. Arthur Jenkins persuaded Clem Attlee to invite Beveridge and myself to dinner at the Oxford and Cambridge Club, in the hope that the two great men, Attlee and Beveridge, who were of the same generation, would cement an alliance. Nothing of the kind, alas, occurred. Beveridge unwisely laid down the law on many matters involved in the running of the war, with which Attlee, Deputy Prime Minister, was too closely concerned to discuss them. He lapsed into almost total silence. Finally, after dinner, he disappeared into the depths of an armchair and fell asleep. By the time he woke, Beveridge had followed his example, leaving Arthur Jenkins and myself to chatter away as best we could. Soon after, the party broke up. Our masters walked along Pall Mall together, Arthur and I following at a respectful distance. Arthur turned to me and said, 'I think it went pretty well, don't you?' Feeling that it could hardly have gone worse, I made no comment. Not long afterwards, Beveridge told me that he had joined the Liberal Party. I shall always think that somehow or other a great chance was lost.

From 1945 to 1951 Attlee was the firm, decisive chairman of a Cabinet that carried through a social revolution without violence or acrimony; moreover, in conjunction with the Americans, it built the whole post-war system of Western defence; it transformed, in Harold Wilson's phrase, 'the British Empire into the Commonwealth of Nations, linked together in common allegiance to the sovereign as head of the Commonwealth'.

Whatever the future holds, the immense improvement in the lot of the poor during the Attlee period of Labour leadership, 1935–55, is beyond question. When I was an Oxford don and a City Councillor for Cowley an elderly man admitted to me that he would like to get more than ten shillings a week, which was then the old-age pension. He had been a friend of Nuffield (then Billy Morris) in the old days. Billy Morris had tried to persuade him to go into motor-cars, but he had said to Billy, 'You'll never beat the horses.' He was now sorry to hear that Lord Nuffield's health was not very good, but his was excellent, so he had no real reason for regret, though he would have liked a little more than ten shillings a week – i.e., £26 a year. Today as an old age pensioner I am drawing at least five times as much in real terms.

Whatever one says about the influence of inflation, there can be no doubt that the lot of the poorest has been improved enormously, and in my estimation the names of Attlee and Beveridge are the most glorious. In the long run, the first had more influence than the second.

It helped matters that he was so conservative in his private tastes. His beloved wife supported him with total dedication, but was always understood to have remained a Conservative. She once said to Kenneth Harris in the late 1950s, 'Most of our friends are Conservative. But you were never really a socialist, were you, darling?' Attlee, sitting next to her, reading *The Times*, pipe in mouth, made a mildly dissenting noise. 'Well, not a rabid one,' she said, by way of finishing the discussion. When I took him in my government car to the country funeral of his old colleague Albert Alexander he was the only man who wore a top hat. 'They call me a Victorian,' he remarked laconically.

I was one of the few aspiring Labour politicians who were defeated in 1945, when I attempted to wrest Oxford from the present Lord Hailsham (then Quintin Hogg). I was feeling very lost after my defeat. I had written to Clem Attlee, whom I had come to know quite well, not of course asking for anything, but expressing general enthusiasm at the Labour victory. In due course a letter arrived from him. It was the first of many in his own hand that I was to receive, all marvellously characteristic, all saying rather less, but meaning rather more, than a similar message from anyone else. This one uplifted me by reference to my fine fight at Oxford, a conventional phrase from anyone else, but from Attlee significant and restoring. It ended by saying that he would want to see me later on. Which again, coming from Attlee, seemed meaningful.

Nothing happened for three weeks – a discreet inquiry produced less than no result. And then came a sudden summons to No. 10 – 'Would you care to help us in the Lords?' 'Oh, yes, yes, I'd help you anywhere,' I found myself saying. 'And there's another point' (a word all men of affairs use unceasingly, but with Attlee, by reason of its very guardedness, a supreme favourite). 'I would like you to speak for the Government as a Lord-in-Waiting. But that will need clearing with the Palace.' I stammered my thanks and started to leave, but he checked my exuberance before I escaped. 'Don't say a word about the Lord-in-Waiting to anyone – except your wife,' he enjoined. The considerate family touch was once again very typical of Clem Attlee. (To see him at his happiest you needed to see him with Mrs Attlee giving a children's party at Christmas.) But the emphasis on security was sufficient to give me a positive complex, perhaps a healthy one, from which I am not yet emancipated.

As a Lord-in-Waiting, as a member of a very small Labour group in the House of Lords, I had exceptional opportunities of speaking for the Government. Clem Attlee encouraged me at all times. In the autumn of 1946, in the course of a general 'reshuffle', I was sent for by No. 10. 'Want you to become Paliamentary Secretary at the Ministry of National Insurance. Should be up your street.' I was out of the room before I had time to formulate any response, but as I walked along Whitehall some inner voice told me that this was not the right appointment for me. It was the obvious one, no doubt. A major bill giving effect to the main ideas of the Beveridge Report would be coming forward. There would be a great chance for me to shine. But I was still bitterly disappointed by my failure to see active service.

Leslie Hore-Belisha, the fallen Secretary of State for War, had said to me at the time, 'If you can't do anything more *in* the Army, perhaps you'll one day do something *for* the Army.' With what seems now extraordinary effrontery, I returned to Downing Street and begged Attlee for a post connected with the Services. He confined himself, as usual, to the smallest possible number of words. 'Let you know later,' and in due course the Prime Minister informed me that I was to be Under-Secretary of State for War.

Was there any special reason why I should find favour in Attlee's eyes, apart from my being a young Christ Church don and therefore a bit of an acquisition? My courtesy title (I was then the Hon. Frank Pakenham) would have made no difference to him. He was certainly no snob in an aristocratic or society sense. But the story told above about his attitude to gentlemanly or non-gentlemanly conduct is revealing. He was happiest with two classes of person: those who had been to good public schools and still cared for public-school values, and those at the other end of the social scale who reflected the community spirit of the working classes at their best. Kenneth Harris tells us that even when he had become a social worker in East London he was still concerned that a glass of claret should be drunk in the right way. But outside his own family the men he came to care for most were probably miners.

He never mentioned my own family to me, but I have always believed that my father's death at Gallipoli created a bias in my favour. Curiously enough, my uncle Arthur Villiers, who had much to do with my upbringing, was born in the same year as Attlee. Like Attlee, he went to work as a young man in the East End. Attlee went on to greatness. My uncle presided over the Eton Manor Club in Hackney Wick, which he and others had founded, for close on fifty years apart from the period of the Great War, in which, like Attlee, he rendered valiant service. Attlee was too reserved to discuss with me his background or mine, but looking back I feel that we had much in common.

In 1947 I was appointed Minister of State for Germany. I am never quite clear why I was offered that post. I had vigorously defended the Government and 'our men on the spot in Germany' in a debate at the end of 1946. I had used, with deep conviction, the expression 'Germany today is a tragic mess, but a mess of her own making'. I suppose it was that latter phrase that led Attlee and Bevin to assess me as basically sound, certainly, a strict Roman Catholic, an anticommunist. My next sentence they perhaps ignored: 'God forgive me, if to say what I have just said is to speak unfairly of a people who are suffering as they are suffering now.'

Be that as it may, I was soon advocating policies based on my interpretation of Christianity and involving equal partnership for Germany. Such policies have long since been accepted, but they were far too pro-German for the Cabinet, and in particular for the Foreign Secretary, Ernest Bevin. They were certainly in conflict with the Potsdam policy, which the four allies, Britain, America, France and Russia, were still nominally carrying out. Bevin, long-suffering towards me, finally burst out: 'The trouble about you is that, though you are Chancellor of the Duchy [pronounced Ducky], you don't agree with my German policy.'

I used to call on Clem Attlee with increasing frequency. Looking back he put up with a lot. He was the greatest of listeners. There was the famous occasion when Dick Crossman spent half an hour denouncing the Government's attitude to Israel. Attlee said nothing, but commented at the end: 'Saw your mother last week.'

I must have been a great disappointment to him, although he never showed it. Then and later, after I had been moved from Germany, I kept on threatening to resign. He had a masterly way of replying to such screeds: 'My dear Frank, Thank you for your note. I will try to see you as soon as possible. Yours ever, Clem.' I learnt my lesson, and nearly twenty years later effected a resignation from a Cabinet without preliminaries.

In later years, after he had ceased to be Prime Minister, Clem Attlee came out strongly against the idea of Britain joining the Common Market. He was at the same time (though now an octogenarian) supplying leadership and inspiration to the movement for world government. He seemed to me at that time to take a rather narrow view of the first matter and a wide, imaginative view of the second. He used to say that he did not like treating the Germans and Italians, whom we had defeated in the war, as more intimate friends than the loyal peoples of the Commonwealth. It was not till then (the 1960s) that I discovered the depth of his antipathy to the Germans. I asked him to be a patron of the Anglo-German Association, of which I was chairman. After a moment's hesitation he broke the news to me that he never could stand Germans. This was, I must suppose, a relic of the First World War attitude. He only made one qualification. 'Vi and I once had a German maid we liked.' This revelation of his anti-Germanism in a sense increases still further my respect for the way he treated me when I was Minister for Germany.

In April 1948 I spent a fortnight at home in Hampstead, recovering from an injured Achilles tendon. One night in particular I slept badly, returning again and again to the problem of resignation from my position as Minister for Germany: how to break loose from a responsibility which I felt unable to share, without damaging my colleagues.

In the morning, at about eleven o'clock, a telephone message reached us at our house to the effect that Mr Attlee wondered if he could call. By the time he arrived the children and household were on parade to greet him, while I attempted to rise from my invalid sofa. After accepting a cup of tea and inquiring about my tendon, he came briskly to the point. 'I think it's about time you had a Department of your own,' he told me. 'I've got Civil Aviation in mind. Harry Nathan has been anxious to return to his business for some time.'

My first feelings, I am bound to record, were those of enormous relief at my escape from a painful dilemma. I promised to give an answer in a few days' time. When the moment came I was much less happy. Was I, I asked, being kicked upstairs? Was I deserting Germany? Had this come about because of disagreement with Mr Bevin? Clem Attlee with a few masterly touches disposed of all these anxieties. It would have been a marked reflection on me not to have received promotion. There would no doubt be opportunities of contributing my views on German affairs. He had all the gentleness of the dove, but was not without the wisdom of the serpent. He could read the human heart, though he would have shrunk from the very idea of possessing psychic intuition.

For three years, as Minister of Civil Aviation, I devoted most of my energies to my departmental job, and much progress in fact was made. It was not a subject in which Clem Attlee took any interest. I was only once brought into 'painful' contact with him in that area. I had exercised my right to set aside the findings of an inquiry into a major air crash. I did it clumsily, and for about twenty-four hours the newspaper headlines made bad reading for my family and myself. 'Pakenham may be asked to resign' (*Evening Standard*). 'Sack for Pakenham' (*Star*). 'Lord Pakenham may go' (*Evening News*).

I was soon on the mat at No. 10. What Attlee was concerned to discover – which was not at first evident – was whether I was within my constitutional rights in turning down the findings of the inquiry. Once he was satisfied on that point, he was determined to back me. But his professional standards were affronted by the clumsiness by which I appeared to have handled the situation. His first question when I was called to his office was simple. 'How can you set up a court and then refuse to accept its decision when it goes against your own men?' I seemed to read into his remarks a conviction that I had violated those ultimate British traditions of which cricket, his adored sport, was the outward symbol. 'The umpire's decision is final.' Once we repudiated that, we would indeed be on a slippery slope.

However, that side of it had now been cleared up. But he read me a sharp lesson on the solidarity required of Ministers. I did not feel that I was restored to his confidence until eighteen months later, when I became First Lord of the Admiralty and a member of the Defence Committee.

On the occasion of that appointment an unusual sense of my unworthiness swept over me, not forgetting my own inglorious war record. 'Please don't think I don't appreciate the honour. No one who has read a line of British history or got any feeling for it could fail to be stirred. But the Navy deserves the best. Its traditions are everything to it. I don't think I am the right sort of person. I mean' – I searched for words – 'I mean, I am too eccentric.'

'I shouldn't worry about that,' replied the Prime Minister, enormously blithe. 'The Navy survived Winston and Brendan – it will probably survive you.' He thought I would prove entirely adequate.

His humility was total. On one occasion after a debate in the House of Lords he and Vi Attlee asked Elizabeth and me to dinner. It emerged with some embarrassment that neither of them knew a restaurant in London. I suppose that he had done most of his entertaining at the Oxford and Cambridge Club, where he was always supposed to have told a member who was unwise enough to tackle him on politics: 'Don't talk shop in Mess!'

I selected a restaurant, not very expensive, near Sloane Square. We had a delightful meal together, but afterwards there was a further moment of embarrassment. He took me aside and asked me if I would mind paying the bill; he would give me his cheque for the amount. 'Afraid they wouldn't know me here.' He had been Prime Minister, he was a Knight of the Garter, possessed the Order of Merit, but he had no more sense of his importance than if he had been some young parliamentary candidate. In his retirement he continued to go home every night by Underground to Great Missenden, indistinguishable from any other commuter of the professional classes.

If I am asked what sort of socialist I have been for the last forty-eight years, I would reply 'an Attlee socialist', though he has now for many years been dead. I am thinking of his policies, of his handling of affairs, and most of all of his character.

It is for me a sobering reflection that the two statesmen I have admired most in this century both made their way to the top without trying to get there. De Valera, my other hero, achieved the leadership of Ireland through the 'accident' of the 1916 rising. It is not disparaging the leaders in later times – Harold Wilson, Ted Heath, James Callaghan and Margaret Thatcher – to suggest that their struggle to the top was as prolonged and purposeful as that of Sebastian Coe or Steve Ovett to an Olympic Gold Medal.

In my eyes Clem Attlee was the most selfless politician of the first rank that I have known, the most ethical Prime Minister in the whole of British history. He lacked the Christian earnestness of Mr Gladstone, but was happily without the latter's power of self-deception. Churchill was great by any known standards and was by no means devoid of moral qualities, but he would hardly be selected as an ethical giant.

I have said that Clem Attlee was selfless, but he was extremely tough and tenacious in defence of his proper rights. No one dislodged him from his leadership, though more than one such attempt was made by aspiring rivals. In his own eyes he was a soldier whose business was to stay in the front line until recalled by high authority.

In the Cabinet he was ready in economic matters to defer to better-informed Cabinet colleagues, though always insisting that the final result must make sense in the eyes of the layman. But in such matters as defence and Commonwealth affairs he had complete faith in his own personal judgment, and authorized the construction of the atom bomb, so far as it is known, without qualms – and certainly without reference to the Cabinet as a whole. In foreign policy it would be hard to distinguish his contribution from that of Ernest Bevin.

Lord Boothby has paid special tribute to his courage, first over Berlin, then over Korea. 'When the Russians tried to occupy the whole of Berlin, he never flinched from the Berlin airlift, which was a brilliant success, and saved the western half of the city. There were to be no more Yaltas under his leadership.' The comparison with Truman is striking. Both emerged from almost total obscurity. One became one of the best peacetime Presidents, and the other the best peacetime Prime Minister the country has had in this century.

Mrs Gandhi has paid tribute to him as 'a man at ease with himself, a man of earnestness, economy and sound commonsense. The condition of Indians was on his conscience.' She leaves us in no doubt that he was a man apart in the story of Indian independence from the British side. 'Lord Attlee', she has written, 'is one of the few to find a place in the history of two countries.' In that perspective, one cannot point to anyone who bears comparison with him.

Of his ethical principles I have spoken above; on his other fundamental beliefs it would be unwise to dogmatize. One would dearly like to claim him as a Christian. Against that there is a piece of dialogue recorded by Kenneth Harris: 'Attlee summed up his attitude this way: "Believe in the ethics of Christianity. Can't believe the mumbo-jumbo."

Harris: "Would you say you are an agnostic?"

Attlee: "I don't know."

Harris: "Is there an after-life, do you think?"

Attlee: "Possibly."'

But Attlee was the first to acknowledge the strength of the Christianity of his parents, brothers and sisters. The fact of his Christian upbringing is not in dispute. He found that his friends tended to be Christians, a good few of them parsons. He chose for his funeral service the famous passage from Ecclesiastes which ends: 'Let us hear the conclusion of the whole matter: Fear God, and keep His commandments: for this is the whole duty of man. For God shall bring every work into judgment, with every secret thing, whether it be good, or whether it is evil.'

It was said of Rosebery that, if not a poet, he was of the stuff that poets delight in. Attlee was indubitably of the stuff that Christians delight in.

Anthony Eden

The Gallant Gentleman

EDEN
Rt Hon. Sir (Robert) Anthony
(1897–1977)

M.P. (C) Warwick and Leamington, 1923–57.

Parliamentary Private Secretary to Secretary of State for Foreign Affairs
(Sir Austen Chamberlain, KG), 1926–9;
Parliamentary Under-Secretary, Foreign Office, 1931–3;
Lord Privy Seal, 1934–5;
Minister without Portfolio for League of Nations Affairs, 1935;
Secretary of State for Foreign Affairs, 1935–8;
for Dominion Affairs, 1939–40;
for War, 1940;
for Foreign Affairs, 1940–5;
also Leader of House of Commons, 1942–5;
Deputy Leader of the Opposition, 1945–51;
Secretary of State for Foreign Affairs and Deputy Prime Minister, 1951–April 1955;
Prime Minister and First Lord of the Treasury, April 1955–January 1957.
K.G. 1954;
Created 1st Earl of Avon, 1961.

The Gallant Gentleman

A S A YOUNG MAN FRESH from Eton, Anthony Eden had endured the rigours of the Western Front in the First World War and proved his manhood for all time. By far the best book he ever wrote, the most artistic and the most revealing, was *Another World, 1897—1917* (his first twenty years), which appeared shortly before his death. He was a younger son of an aristocratic landowner in County Durham who was deeply versed in modern painting and to whom George Moore had recently dedicated a book of essays on that subject. Eden from boyhood was a great lover of the arts; he can write modestly of his later taste:

> We all date somewhere. I am conscious that I do myself. Most abstract art is a closed book to me and, while I consider Picasso one of the greatest draughtsmen of all time, and his Blue Period among the world's finest painting, I cannot feel quite the same towards some of his later work, particularly the colour. It is on this account that, of the two cubist founders, I generally prefer Braque of the twenties and thirties.

This sensitive youth steeled himself to endure every horror. He was the adjutant of his battalion at nineteen, and a brigade major at twenty. What price he had to pay internally one can guess at. His courage in politics as in war was at all times unlimited, but his stamina became suspect in many eyes, including mine.

In 1950 I spoke with him at a big United Nations rally in the grounds of Warwick Castle, the home of his nephew. After a champagne lunch, though I did not notice whether he imbibed, we repaired to the garden and sat there under the blazing sun. There were various speeches, including mine (I was Minister for Civil Aviation at the time, he was Deputy Leader of the Opposition). By the time his turn came, he must have been affected by the heat. He began well enough, amid rapturous applause, but at a certain moment he faltered. 'I well remember during my recent tour in Australia . . . I well remember during my recent tour in Australia' — suddenly he pitched forward and fell on the grass beside me. He rose without a moment's hesitation and began again. 'I well remember during my recent tour in Australia . . .' his voice faded away. This time, as he fell, I was at least aware enough to catch him. He was a tall, well-made man, but I was astonished that he was so light. For a very brief moment he was unconscious. Then he rose again, murmuring to me, 'Sorry to be such a bore, Frank, I think they want to hear me – I can't let them down,' and was proposing to continue his speech indomitably.

Mercifully, Lord Warwick intervened. But that was not the end of Anthony Eden's day. After tea he set off to make two more speeches in the neighbourhood. He was in excellent form at dinner. Next morning he left early for yet one more series of speaking engagements. I said to myself at the time: Here is a man who will at all times in the course of duty press himself to the limit and beyond the limit of his physical strength. To quote something that Tom Brown's father said to Tom Brown, when the latter set off for Rugby: 'Never give in while you can stand or see.'

Anthony Eden will always remain the supreme might-have-been of British Prime Ministers. Speculation about the might-have-beens of high-level politics is tantalizing and inevitably inconclusive. If Hugh Gaitskell had lived, it is almost certain that he would have been Prime Minister instead of Harold Wilson, when Labour came back to power in 1964. Old friends like myself and many others believed that he would have been a great Prime Minister. But he would have had to acquire an increased tolerance of those who disagreed with him inside and outside his party. There were signs that he was moving in this direction, at the time of his tragic death. Well-informed friends of Iain Macleod make the same hypothetical claims for him. He was struck down within a few weeks of becoming Chancellor of the Exchequer under Ted Heath in 1970. He had not the intellectual background or economic expertise of Hugh Gaitskell, though one must not underestimate the mental powers of one of the finest bridge-players of his generation. Hugh Gaitskell was firmer on principles. Macleod had more natural flair for mass communication.

Anthony Eden's premiership ended in disaster. His own health broke down totally, and the Suez adventure was an admitted catastrophe. Who can say what he would have done when Nasser nationalized the Canal if his health had been normal? Who can say whether his health would have been adequate for the incredibly strenuous role of Prime Minister if he had come to power earlier – if Churchill had not kept him waiting so long? Churchill's attitude towards him remains enigmatic. There is no reason to doubt the truth of Churchill's account of his own feelings when Eden resigned in February 1938. For once sleep deserted him. The one gallant light in the murk of the Government had been extinguished; darkness pervaded all. For a moment an ultimate pessimism threatened the indomitable soul.

Churchill has put on record that when he undertook arduous wartime journeys he left a recommendation that if anything happened to him he could be succeeded by Eden. Nevertheless, he was so anxious to stay in office himself that he began to obtain a mischievous pleasure from the thought of Eden waiting on the doorstep. My friend Raymond Blackburn, who entered Parliament in 1945 as a young Labour MP of immense promise, was taken up by Churchill. Raymond took his father, a doctor, on a visit to Churchill at Chartwell. Dr Blackburn looked at Churchill in admiration and amazement, Churchill then being in his early seventies. 'You'll live to be a hundred,' he predicted. Churchill replied, with a twinkle, 'You'd better tell that to Anthony Eden.'

It is doubtful whether Eden would ever have been able to sustain indefinitely the incredible burdens of the office of Prime Minister. Lord Home, PPS to Chamberlain before the war, may be slightly biased in favour of the latter, but he is the most objective and honest of narrators. He has written:

> Eden, trained under Austen Chamberlain, was the accomplished diplomat, popular at home and patient, persuasive and flexible in his contacts with foreign statesmen. He had an almost unfair ration of charm, and if occasionally there appeared a touch of vanity there was certainly a lot which could be put to his credit while still a young man.

Nothing very damaging there. But in a later passage he describes Eden's relationship with Neville Chamberlain painfully:

> Eden was temperamental and lived on his nerves, while Chamberlain's reaction to a crisis of personal relations was an icy and forbidding calm. On the last occasion that I staged a meeting, Eden had a streaming cold, and as he came into the room Chamberlain looked up and told him to go and take two aspirins, and to come back in the morning when he would make more sense.

The fact that Eden could be treated so disdainfully indicates that at that time Neville Chamberlain regarded him as a lightweight, a young man in any case not much more than half his own age. It is inconceivable that at that time Eden, still under forty, could have taken over the whole future of Britain.

From Anthony Eden's point of view it would no doubt have been best if Churchill had retired in 1945. Eden, however, it must be remembered, had been able to play virtually no part in the General Election. He had been prostrated with nervous exhaustion following the immense strain of the war. During the war years he had played a part of incalculable value as Foreign Secretary which places him in the highest bracket of the men who brought us victory. Whether his health would at any time have stood the supreme strain of the premiership must be problematical.

The peaks and the abysses lie close together in politics. Ten Prime Ministers died in the seven decades after Campbell-Bannerman: Balfour, Asquith, Lloyd George, Bonar Law, Ramsay MacDonald, Chamberlain, Baldwin, Churchill, Attlee, Eden (by then Lord Avon). Apart from Bonar Law – Prime Minister for only a few months before his death – Attlee and Churchill, each of the others was by the end a rejected man. Several were utterly discredited in the minds of the multitude.

Curzon was overcome with grief when Baldwin was made Prime Minister. But by 1940, after the fall of France, as I have recounted earlier, Baldwin was crying out, 'Why do they hate me so?' Yet this was the same British public which a few years before had responded to his lightest touch, and at the time of the Abdication had hailed him as a veritable wizard. To a greater or lesser extent, the others underwent a like experience.

Anthony Eden was a national hero before he was forty, the youngest man to occupy such a position in politics since Rosebery. He became Foreign Secretary at the end of 1935, at the age of thirty-eight, imposed as it were on the old men by the voice of the people. Nearly forty years later, David Owen was to become Foreign Secretary at the same age. He also was tall, dark and handsome, and a fine parliamentarian. But he found his way to this exalted position through the accident of the death of Tony Crosland. He had no national standing to compare with that of Eden in the 1930s.

When Eden resigned in February 1938 – that is, a little over two years after his appointment – he consolidated his glory. I have already quoted what Churchill said about his own feelings of gloom and distress at that time. On the other hand, we in the Oxford Labour Party were thrilled. Eden was symbolic of something indefinably noble. It is right that he should always be remembered as the young statesman who stood out for the vision which had inspired the establishment of the League of Nations. Forty years, therefore, before his death Eden became a national institution. Such he remained in the eyes of the public. I did not realize this fully until I became a Knight of the Garter and took part in the annual procession at Windsor. The Knights proceeded in reverse order of seniority. A ripple of applause would greet each of us as we passed along.

Suddenly, way back, one heard a tremendous roar – it was the public recognizing their old favourite Anthony Eden.

Eden may or may not have been – as has been said quite often – a man of few intimate friends. Those who make these assertions are seldom qualified to judge. His private life had been troubled. His first wife departed to America. In his second marriage he encountered a sublime devotion fully returned. Few would have expected him to live for long after his breakdown in health at the time of Suez. Clarissa Churchill, as she was when I first knew her, sustained him through another twenty years of married happiness. On their part, the public saw him down the years, Suez or no Suez, as the incarnation of charm and popularity.

Nor did this fabulous popularity derive from a low or purely superficial appeal. No doubt in the early years there was the Eden homburg hat and the trouser-creases. Then and later, his handsome face and lithe figure were a major asset. He never lost the feel in his antennae which made him a platform draw. He seldom, if ever, disappointed his great audiences, though he never possessed – or at any rate never exhibited in public – any particular gift of phrase. Churchill is supposed to have said that one of his speeches contained every cliché in the language except, 'Please adjust your clothing on leaving the toilet.' His cultural life was reserved for his intimates. But he stood for something which weighed much more heavily than culture.

For twenty-five years Eden was felt to represent the highest common denominator of British political conviction on the greatest international issues. He was considered, with reason, to be a man who like Baldwin had been capable of seeing the good points of his opponents, and putting country before party. (Which was how Baldwin was regarded in pre-war days.)

When Eden first emerged, when I first met him at the Astors' house, Cliveden, in the 1930s, he had the extraordinary aura of a man with unique double credentials. He had been a front-line fighter in the war; he was a patriot by the most exacting standards. But he was also the young man with a 'frightening passion for peace', according to a French Prime Minister. His championship of the League of Nations appeared as fanatical as that of Lord Robert Cecil himself.

The 1938 resignation finally stamped this image of him on the public mind. If today one concludes that Chamberlain forced him into resignation, that does not detract from the stand that he was making in the Cabinet for his principles. It would have been an impossible responsibility without his first-class professional competence, his mastery of international questions and the public character which had nothing to conceal. He was not equipped with any outstanding powers of reflection or far-sighted imagination, or even their verbal substitutes. He will not be remembered for any long-term projections as will Ernest Bevin. But his ideals were sound, his instincts appropriate to the time. Whatever his limitations, he never lacked the courage to stand for what he believed to be right. If it be possible, he had that quality in excess, or at least in too simplified a form.

Twice only since the end of the First World War have the people of Britain been split from top to bottom over foreign policy. Once in 1936–9 and once over Suez. In the earlier phase Eden resigned – all honour to him. But the clean cut, the breach with his colleagues, did not come naturally to him. He remained Foreign Secretary while sanctions against Italy were abandoned, and when he did leave the Government he made little fuss or impact until the war enforced national unity.

By 1956 a cleavage was steadily revealing itself in Britain between the imperial and the United Nations conceptions of policy. There was still a hankering after the past glories of the Empire and more immediate hopes pinned on peace through the United Nations than exist in the United Kingdom in the 1980s. Eden seemed to procrastinate, as well he might if the country were to be held together. His own party began to mutter and rumble, finding personal points of criticism which had previously been overlooked. An influential writer in the *Daily Telegraph*, my wife's brother-in-law Donald McLachlan, called for 'the smack of firm government', pointing out that the characteristic gesture of Eden was to bring down his fist without striking the palm of the other hand. No one, however, questioned his diplomatic talents or power to represent a united people. 'They may say he is weak,' said an intimate of his to a friend of mine, just before Colonel Nasser nationalized the Suez Canal company, 'but he will never do anything to divide our people. He remembers the pre-war débâcle too clearly.'

Ironic words. A month later we were all at one another's throats. Nasser nationalized the Suez Canal, an act of defiance which led Eden to see him as a latter-day Hitler who must be destroyed at all costs. Harold Macmillan in his memoirs has put this point of view more clearly even than Eden. He writes:

> The unanimous view of my colleagues was in favour of strong and resolute action. . . it was clear that Nasser was determined to throw his weight in favour of revolution and Arab expansion with the help of

Communist intrigue and supported by Communist money and arms. With a jealous eye on the oil-bearing countries, he was determined to pursue an aggressive policy on lines of which we had only too recent and too painful experience.

International pressures were promoted but Eden, supported by Macmillan and others in his inner circle, made preparations from the beginning for a military solution. They pressed on regardless of the hostility of the American Government whose reactions they had totally miscalculated. The United Nations and, speaking generally, the Commonwealth were ignored or flouted. A collusive plan was entered into with France and Israel under which Israel would invade Egypt and Britain and France be given an excuse to intervene. At the end of October, three months after the nationalization of the Canal, the invasions took place, but under world pressure – more particularly that of the United States, with the consequent run on the pound – the whole adventure had to be abandoned. Eden, already in wretched health, withdrew for a holiday to Ian Fleming's house Golden Eye in the Caribbean. On his return he handed in his resignation on medical advice to the Queen.

Some critics saw all this as folly in *realpolitik* terms. Others, not least Hugh Gaitskell, castigated the flouting of the United Nations; others again could not stomach the humbug and hypocrisy, the collusion, the high-minded pretence that the Anglo-French intervention was a peace operation, designed to put out the fire of war and separate the combatants, Egypt and Israel. In fact, it was the self-appointed firemen who had themselves lit the fire, by secretly arranging the Israeli attack on Sinai.

Was it accident that Eden, the supreme diplomatist, the lifelong exponent of negotiated settlement, the unifier *par excellence*, should finish up as the strong-arm pundit, the great divider – and not of his country only? One cause, no doubt, was his desire to unite his party behind his leadership, as mentioned above. The right-wing Tories had long been criticizing him for being too weak. But here comes in the imponderable health factor. If he had still possessed the strength and buoyancy of his best days, one feels that he would have refrained from military intervention until he had worked up some support for it in the rest of the world. He would surely have never proceeded without far more backing from the United States and the Commonwealth.

For myself, I am confident that he could never have united the country, or carried the Labour Party with him, in any policy which flagrantly defied the United Nations. Equally, there is no doubt that his intervention made him considerably more popular with his own side than for a long while previously, and as far as these things can be measured, with public opinion in the short run. The public only came slowly to understand what a shocking mistake it was.

It has been said that an orator must be what his age would have him be, or else not be at all. Eden, though no orator, was heroically resolved to be loyal to public opinion. This seemed to him to be in harmony with the policy of resisting dictators which had first brought him to honourable prominence in the 1930s. However, he had never been a man to *lead* public opinion, and by the middle 1950s the pre-war attitudes for good or for ill were out of date.

'How unlike him', was the general comment from many who knew him well, when he acted so drastically, so unexpectedly and with such fatal results over Suez. In fact, his legacy of thought and feeling had expired. A situation had emerged for which he had no prepared values and no inner source of fresh inspiration. Technique and faithfulness and courage were not enough. His life's dream of national harmony behind a British moral leadership of pre-war pattern in international affairs had faded irretrievably. 'The captain', as Sir Winston Churchill said of Woodrow Wilson, 'went down with the ship.' As one always knew he would if the situation arose.

His later years were much taken up with his memoirs. They were not greeted with much enthusiasm, except for the volume dealing with his early years. This won universal approval. There were many glimpses of the artist concealed for so many years under the statesman. These were years of dignity and detachment. Earlier memories were revived of the national rather than the party statesman. The public maintained a warm place for him in their hearts.

I remember him speaking in the House of Lords on the Common Market, which by no means appealed to him. Many who had seen little of him for years marvelled at the distinction of his looks, enhanced rather than impaired by years of suffering and evident frailty, and his still unrivalled charm.

Playing sensitively on the feelings of the audience, he gently but unmistakably guided us along a different line from that of his own front bench. It was exquisitely done. 'Truly,' I said to myself, 'one does not become Prime Minister by accident.'

On the other hand, it may be that one does not remain Prime Minister for very long without a certain kind of insensitivity not possessed by Anthony Eden.

Harold Macmillan

The Masterly Man

MACMILLAN
Rt Hon. (Maurice) Harold
(1894–   )

M.P. (U) Stockton-on-Tees, 1924–9 and 1931–45;
M.P. (C) Bromley, November 1945–September 1964.

Parliamentary Secretary, Ministry of Supply, 1940–2;
Parliamentary Under-Secretary of State, Colonies, 1942;
Minister Resident at Allied HQ in North-West Africa, 1942–5;
Secretary for Air, 1945;
Minister of Housing and Local Government, 1951–4;
Minister of Defence, October 1954–April 1955;
Secretary of State for Foreign Affairs, April–December 1955;
Chancellor of the Exchequer, December 1955–January 1957;
Prime Minister and First Lord of the Treasury, January 1957–October 1963.
Created 1st Earl of Stockton, 1984.

The Masterly Man

Harold Macmillan began and ended his premiership in an atmosphere of 'medical' drama. One cannot say when the idea entered his mind that Eden's health might collapse, and he himself be called on to take his place. It was not so very long since he had talked of retiring to the Lords and claiming the earldom which he considered his due. When he attained the age of ninety, twenty-one years after he had ceased to be Prime Minister, he received an earldom amid general acclaim. In 1963 it was ironic that he, who had so boldly espoused the Suez adventure, should be preferred to Butler, who had shown himself very ambivalent. There was no doubt at all that the Cabinet overwhelmingly preferred Macmillan.

Six and a half years later he was showing an uncharacteristic indecisiveness in trying to make up his mind whether to resign or stay on and fight the next election. On 7 October he finally made up his mind to stay on as Prime Minister. Twenty-four hours later, he was in King Edward VII Hospital awaiting an urgent operation for a serious inflammation of the prostate gland. It had seemed that if he did indeed retire he would nominate Lord Hailsham as his successor. When the time came he threw his weight emphatically behind Lord Home. It is arguable though by no means certain that Home would have been in any case elected, but it was Macmillan who made sure that this would occur.

Harold Macmillan had 'what it takes' to be Prime Minister. He came to the premiership at an appalling moment for Britain. It was the morrow of Suez and the national humiliation that that involved. British prestige was at a low ebb. So was our special relationship with the United States. The morale of the Conservative Party was if possible lower still. Yet before long everything was restored, our status in the world, our relationship with America and Conservative self-confidence.

The best book so far about Harold Macmillan is by Nigel Fisher, formerly one of his junior Ministers. He treats the first part of Macmillan's 6½-year reign as highly successful, the last half as a period of relative decline. With all these Prime Ministers – usually old when they enter office, and some years older by the time they finish – we are left to speculate about the influence of declining health, or at any rate declining vigour. Macmillan was undoubtedly a tired man by the end of his premiership, although twenty years later he could entrance an audience of Rhodes Scholars by addressing them for an hour without a note.

Harold Wilson in his book *A Prime Minister on Prime Ministers* ends the essay on Macmillan by saying:

> Few Prime Ministers have worked so hard, and even fewer derived so much enjoyment from it. Few have had so wide-ranging a grip on every aspect of government, or so clear – or so easy – a command over their colleagues. Few rivalled his sense of history, few felt as identified as he was with that history and, of those who did, even fewer savoured the challenges, the tasks and the protocol as much as he did.

By and large, the assessment is fully justified.

In one interesting respect, Macmillan's career has been the opposite of Eden's. If Eden had never been Prime Minister, he would have gone down to history as a highly successful Foreign Secretary. In this century I would rank him next after Ernest Bevin. He lacked Bevin's imaginative foresight, but was an even more skilful diplomatist. The part he played in the war entitles him to rank as one of the half-dozen men who contributed most to victory. But his short period as Prime Minister was, as we have seen, disastrous.

Harold Macmillan was born in 1894, the son of a leading publisher whose father, himself the son of a poor crofter, had founded the famous and wealthy firm. His mother was an American, like the mothers of Winston Churchill and Lord Hailsham. She had been a fine singer, and bestirred herself as actively as Churchill's mother in promoting Harold's advancement.

His high level of intelligence was evident from early days. He won the third scholarship at Eton, but was compelled by delicate health to leave at the age of fifteen. In later years his stamina was phenomenal. Coached by the pre-eminent classical scholar Ronald Knox and others, he won an Exhibition to Balliol. There he obtained a First in Honour Moderations. It is likely that but for the war he would have followed it by a First in Greats and the presidency of the Oxford Union. His rather elaborate epigrammatic style was already in evidence. His war record was as gallant as that of Anthony Eden but less fortunate. He was wounded according to himself three times, five times according to others. He spent most of the last two years of the war in hospital. Ever afterwards he was no stranger to pain.

He did not return to Oxford after the war. 'There were too many ghosts' (too many friends slaughtered in the holocaust). He became active in the family firm of publishers, and over the years made a large contribution to its continued progress. Through the influence of his mother he became an ADC to the Duke of Devonshire, Governor-General of Canada. In due course he married the Duke's daughter, Lady Dorothy Cavendish, and began his long-enchanted if ambivalent relationship with the higher aristocracy. Meanwhile the idea of 'poping' (joining the Catholic Church), which he had seriously entertained when his friend and tutor Ronnie Knox took that step had been abandoned. But his friendship with Knox never wavered. He welcomed him at Downing Street when Knox, dying of cancer, was on his way to Oxford to deliver the Romanes Lecture. As he saw him into the train at Paddington he said to him, 'I hope you have a good journey.' Knox replied, 'It's rather a long journey, I am afraid.' 'I know you are well prepared,' were Harold Macmillan's last words to his old friend.

He stood for Stockton-on-Tees in 1923 and was narrowly defeated. He stood again in 1924 and won, was defeated in 1929, victorious in 1931, and defeated in the Labour landslide of 1945. Later he was returned at Bromley. The influence of his years as MP or candidate for Stockton was profound: an antidote, if one likes, to the temptations of a view from Chatsworth or the board of a great publishing company. He has himself referred to the humility based on sympathy and understanding that came from his prolonged connection with a distressed area. He certainly acquired a lifelong hatred of mass unemployment; the economics associated with Mrs Thatcher could not conceivably have been his.

In the 1930s he won a reputation for independence of thought and action. Yet he had never held even the most trivial office till Churchill came to power in 1940. By that time Macmillan was already forty-six. Nor was this due to his entering Parliament late like Neville Chamberlain, who was forty-eight when he arrived at Westminster. Macmillan was in Parliament from 1924 onwards with the one break from 1929 to 1931.

As time went on his independence was, no doubt, one reason why he was not made a Minister. He resigned the Conservative Whip for the last year of Baldwin's administration (1936–7). He felt that the Government by abandoning sanctions against Italy were breaking the promises made at the General Election. (He resumed the Whip when Neville Chamberlain took over.) It was during the Oxford by-election, however, which happened to follow the Munich agreement, that he committed an act of extreme defiance. He spoke for Dr Lindsay, the Master of Balliol, his much-loved college, who stood as an anti-Munich candidate against the Conservative Quintin Hogg (now Lord Hailsham). As one of the active promoters of Lindsay's candidature I welcomed Macmillan's appearance on the scene, but his national stature at that time was not comparable with that of Eden.

Macmillan was opposed to appeasement. However, as he has himself pointed out, he was mainly concerned during the 1930s with social and economic questions. In the General Election of 1935 he had fought a distinctly independent campaign. He based his policies on a manifesto called *The Next Five Years*, which he had partly drafted and which had the support of a wide range of public figures of all parties. Horrifying to orthodox Tories, it included recommendations for public control of transport, gas and electricity, nationalization of the Bank of England, the abolition of the means test and an increase in death duties. He carried these ideas still further in his book *The Middle Way*, which appeared in 1938.

To quote Nigel Fisher: 'Although he was well aware of the weaknesses of the capitalist system Macmillan believed that they could be corrected by a measure of government intervention and that this was far preferable to the imposition of full-blooded socialism.' Macmillan is entitled to claim that he has remained true to the advocacy of a middle position, and also, it may be added, of a high degree of national unity, especially in times of crisis.

He was haunted throughout these years by the crushing unemployment which dominated the life of his constituency in Stockton. The Keynesian doctrine of financial expansion, of spending our way out of a depression, made an enormous appeal to him. In all the positions he came to occupy he clung to the vision of full employment. When he was Chancellor of the Exchequer his officials used to make bets as to how often he would mention Stockton, which had long ceased to be his constituency.

When he was Prime Minister he dismissed the resignation of his Chancellor of the Exchequer and two other Treasury ministers in 1957 as 'a little local difficulty'. They had tried to curb public expenditure too sharply for his liking. Five years later he found Selwyn Lloyd too deflationary a Chancellor. He was so anxious to get rid of him that he found it necessary to dismiss six other Cabinet ministers at the same time.

It was this Keynesism, along with other personal factors, which attracted him to Oswald Mosley. In summer 1930 Mosley had just resigned from the Labour Government, demanding a much more positive attack on unemployment. He was at that time the hero of the hour among younger politicians of all parties. I remember sitting next to him after dinner at Cliveden, the Astors' house, and in spite of my youthful academic scepticism, being spellbound. 'After Peel comes Disraeli, after Baldwin and MacDonald comes . . .' Mosley paused, but the implication was clear enough.

Macmillan has never concealed his political intimacy with Mosley during this period. At the time he wrote a long letter to *The Times* expressing general sympathy – a letter, incidentally, for which he was immediately rebuked in the same paper by another rising Conservative MP, closer to the Establishment, called R. A. Butler. In his book *The Pastmasters* Macmillan has written: 'I had then many conversations with Mosley and was struck by his acute intelligence and energy. Indeed I might have been tempted to join his New Party if I could have seen any practical hope of his success.'

As time went on his thinking became bolder still. Fisher quotes a story told by the late and much respected James Margach, a most experienced *Sunday Times* lobby correspondent. According to Margach, Attlee on one occasion described Macmillan as 'by far the most radical man I've known in politics. If it hadn't been for the war, he'd have joined the Labour Party. . . . If that had happened . . . Macmillan would have been Labour's Prime Minister and not me. . . . He was a left-wing radical in his social, human and economic thinking. . . .'

Myself, I do not believe that Attlee said anything that went as far as this. During the late 1930s, I was in touch with Macmillan, apart from the Lindsay by-election, for no more than forty-eight hours, but I have a very clear recollection of our prolonged discussions. I was his fellow-guest in a very small house party at Compton Place, the house of his wife's brother, the then Duke of Devonshire. We had time to play four rounds of golf. The Duke of Devonshire liked his guests to stay up until 4 a.m. over the port, though Harold Macmillan was wise enough to retire to bed long before I did.

I well remember Harold Macmillan discussing in an academic kind of way the question of his joining the Labour Party, but I also remember vividly his conclusion: 'Can I really see myself in the same *galère* as your wild men of the Left? After all, I must remember that I am a very rich man.' It has never crossed my mind that he was referring there to a conflict between his own personal financial interests and socialist policy. He obviously felt sure that with his background and social tastes he would not fit in to the Labour Party as he had come to know it.

Incidentally, his attitude to the aristocracy had always been peculiar in one who was married to a duke's daughter for forty-six years, till her much lamented death in 1966. In a revealing essay on the Whig tradition he reveals a strong *penchant* for great noblemen, especially dukes. Forty years after my visit to Compton Place, he and I were luncheon guests of our old friend Lord Gage at Firle Place. When the time came to go into lunch Harold Macmillan began to insist that the 'nobility' represented by myself should go in first. Of course, I could not acquiesce and he led the way into lunch with one of his charming gestures. Incidentally, he is about the only master of gesture left in public life. I cannot think of anyone else who would have spoken like that – not quite in jest – about the nobility. Quintin Hailsham, every bit as proud as Macmillan of being a professional man, would never have performed such an act of seeming deference to the hereditary aristocracy. I am quite sure that there was never any serious question of Macmillan joining the Labour Party. I am equally sure that there has always been a great gulf fixed between his ideas of economic and social policy and those of Margaret Thatcher. If one had to point to a Conservative Prime Minister whose ideas were similar to hers it would have to be Neville Chamberlain.

Macmillan by the time he reached No. 10 in January 1957 had for short periods been Minister for Defence, Foreign Secretary and Chancellor of the Exchequer. He had made no great mark in any of these posts. He would have liked to have stayed on as Foreign Secretary, but was not sure enough of his ground to insist.

If he had retired to the Lords at that point, as he talked of doing, he would have left little mark on history. At the time he became Prime Minister, he was not a figure well known to the general public, with whom Eden had for twenty years been a great favourite. Macmillan had done splendid work as Minister of State in Africa during the war, and later as Minister of Housing. However, his reputation stood much higher among insiders than it did with the masses, except in so far as they were grateful for his housing achievements. It needed the premiership to give him the historical significance which seemed up to the last moment most unlikely to come his way.

What of his performance as Prime Minister? On the economic front, as mentioned earlier, he clung persistently to the ideal of full employment, and I am not one who will quarrel with him there. It is now recognized that up to 1970, a period covering the Macmillan premiership and that of Wilson from 1964 to 1970, world conditions made progress relatively easy among the industrial nations of the West. Britain progressed more slowly than her rivals, but more rapidly than at any previous time in our history. It is difficult to distinguish the personal achievement of Prime Ministers such as Macmillan and Wilson. Macmillan was entitled to say to the British public in 1959, 'You've never had it so good'; Wilson could have pointed to the still higher standard of living a few years later. Will the economics of Macmillan, with their emphasis on expansion, or those of Mrs Thatcher, which have concentrated on the war against inflation, prove more successful by a purely economic criterion? I remain convinced that Macmillan's social philosophy is much the more humane.

Turning to foreign and commonwealth affairs, his relationship with President Kennedy was in its way a triumph. It was an inspiration – if in retrospect an obvious one – to appoint as Ambassador to Washington his nephew David Ormsby-Gore, an intimate friend of the Kennedy family. The uncle–nephew relationship developed between Macmillan and Kennedy was of indubitable benefit to the Western Alliance, not least during the Cuba crisis of 1962.

Macmillan's record in regard to Europe is somewhat equivocal. He was an early supporter of the European idea after the war, but when Foreign Secretary he allowed himself to be subdued by Eden, who was markedly hostile. When he became Prime Minister he made rather belated efforts to join 'The Six', being duly snubbed by de Gaulle, as was Wilson later. Our eventual entry under the leadership of Edward Heath in 1973 must be held to owe something to Macmillan's initiative.

In the development of the New Commonwealth and the movement of its members to independence he holds an honoured position. His proclamation of a 'wind of change' when visiting South Africa is the best known of all his utterances after 'You've never had it so good'. His own elegant and old-fashioned style reassured Conservatives, while his Government quietly led a retreat from our former position of imperial dominance.

The one serious blot on his whole record is his performance over Suez. Eden must no doubt take the prime responsibility, but Eden, as already mentioned, was a very sick man. Macmillan, who backed him up enthusiastically, had not that excuse. Macmillan was 'first in and first out', as Wilson and others have commented. Unlike Eden, he at least saw when the game was up and, reverting to his shrewd business role, played the dominant part in cutting our losses after the operation failed.

Macmillan's handling of the Profumo affair is sometimes said to have precipitated his own resignation. Certainly it was 'never bright confident morning again', as a Conservative critic bitterly flung at him. Knowing as I do at first hand the magnificent work that Jack Profumo has done in the East End since that time, I try to persuade myself that it has all been for the best. But Jack Profumo and his devoted wife went through great suffering which might have been averted if Macmillan had acted more promptly.

I am ready to believe that Macmillan felt inhibited about discussing a sexual issue with a younger Minister. When I was writing my book on President Kennedy, Macmillan invited me to call on him at his home, Birch Grove. We discussed President Kennedy's visit to him in 1963, and he showed me the rocking chair specially constructed by the Ministry of Works to ease the pain in the President's back. Incidentally, Kennedy looked so ill that Macmillan never expected to see him again. It so happened that there was a story in the newspapers that day to the effect that Kennedy had insisted that regular sex should be provided during the visit. If he didn't have sex every day he got a headache. Harold Macmillan dismissed this absurd supposition with an incomparable gesture. 'Jack wasn't like that. Jack had beautiful manners. He would never have discussed such a matter with me. It would have been like talking about sex to one's father.'

Fisher tells us that Macmillan loved his wife always. 'But his attitude to other women has always been detached. He does not really like them or feel at ease in their company, although this has become less pronounced in recent years.' Nevertheless, I remember his sister-in-law, the Duchess of Devonshire, answering a question of mine as to who was the most effective parliamentary candidate she had ever known with the single word 'Harold'. Harold Macmillan is a shy man, but not a few shy men are happiest when taken out of themselves in the hurly-burly of the hustings or the strange encounters on the electoral doorstep.

In August 1963 the Test Ban Treaty was signed, reflecting much credit on the Prime Minister and the Foreign Secretary, Lord Home. However, by that time he was showing a strange uncertainty as to whether to retire or carry on. The need for a sudden operation settled that issue for him, and not in the way that he would have wished. The resulting struggle for the Conservative leadership must have been distasteful to him. In the end the new Prime Minister, Alec Home, was undoubtedly the one in whom he felt most confidence. He was determined that Butler should not succeed him. He was convinced that Butler lacked sufficient 'steel'. It was not surprising that Butler, his family and friends were left with a persistent bitterness.

Butler was a man of high intellectual talent. Academically he was at least the equal of Macmillan. He possessed, like the latter, a far-reaching political imagination with a deep-rooted devotion to the Conservative Party which Macmillan at no time possessed. Butler's sense of humour was incorrigible and disconcerting. The most famous 'Rabism' was his remark about Anthony Eden: 'The best Prime Minister we've got'. But I enjoyed (afterwards) his remark to me after I had delivered the Address at Freddie Birkenhead's memorial service. 'Very good, of course. It is a pity they don't put in microphones here. I could hear perfectly – but then I was in the front row.' We shall never know now whether he could have produced the hardness and decisiveness required in a national leader. Earlier, perhaps; but not by 1963 in my judgment.

I must turn to Macmillan's personal style, now justly famous. Nigel Fisher says of him: 'As a speaker, Harold Macmillan is in the highest class.' But that was certainly not true of him in the 1930s, or true beyond argument until he became Prime Minister. Fisher himself quotes Tom Jones, secretary to several Prime Ministers, as putting quite a number of young Conservative politicians ahead of Macmillan in 1931. Jones described Macmillan as 'quite able, but I think rather pedestrian', and that is how he continued to appear. Everyone was aware that he was high-minded, courageous and full of constructive thoughts. But he was ponderous, over-elaborate and somewhat artificial in manner. It may have been his rimless glasses, later discarded, which led an aristocratic relative of his wife to compare him to the Austrian Chancellor Schuschnigg. (But what's wrong with rimless glasses? At one time I wore them myself.)

Alastair Horne, in his introduction to an excellent book by Ruth Dudley-Edwards, has a revealing passage, inspired in him by a study of the family album of photographs. He mentions Macmillan as a late developer, and continues:

> The 'Supermac' image was, in fact, but a glaze on the portrait, achieved only after a lifelong struggle against innate diffidence, insecurity and sometimes acute depression. It took me a long time to believe that, even as PM, he would sometimes be physically sick with nerves on the day preceding a major speech. But it was quite true. . . .

This last point fits in with what I have observed. In 1950 or thereabouts I spoke with him (I a Minister, he then in Opposition) at a dinner in Birmingham. My wife sat next to him and noted that during the meal he ate nothing. He kept correcting and recorrecting his script. Horne points out, however, that

> After he became Prime Minister, somewhere between the triumphant Commonwealth tour of 1958 and the equally triumphant general election of 1959, a new self-confident Macmillan appears on the scene. The first incumbent of No 10 to emerge as a TV personality had arrived.

One can trace three developments here: his own powers, including those of entertainment, expanded notably; his self-confidence increased; and what was appropriate in a Prime Minister would have seemed exaggerated in a lesser mortal.

Certainly in later years he delighted many audiences, public and private. I have heard him talking at more than one dining club in such fascinating style that I could have listened to him for hours. However, if he had not been Prime Minister he would hardly have been encouraged to indulge in those splendid monologues. His style would not have been suitable to anyone who had not held the highest office in the State. A phrase from Virginia Woolf's *Orlando* comes back to me: 'Success prompts to exertion and habit facilitates success.'

On one occasion I had taken the chair for him and sat beside him at the annual dinner of the Anglo-German Association. I had drawn, as I thought, a happy comparison between Harold Macmillan the Balliol scholar, the old Guards officer, the prominent businessman, and another principal guest, Herbert Morrison, the man of the people. Harold Macmillan, when he rose to reply, described me with a dramatic uplift of the hands as one who had risen to great heights 'as university don, Minister and great socialist intellectual'. Now I had descended – dropping his hands with the words – 'to the life of a banker'. Happy though not unkind laughter at my expense all round. (I have never since questioned his powers of histrionic ridicule.)

Macmillan never tires of stressing the influence of his American mother. I myself only once heard him speak of her, but then unforgettably. On one occasion, when he was visiting America, he was asked to preach in a conventicle in Indiana. 'I paused on entry', he said, 'for quite a while.' Lloyd George had taught him the value of the pause.

> I looked round the church. I threw up my arms: 'I have been here before,' I told them solemnly. They looked incredulous. They knew that in the ordinary sense this could not be true. But soon they understood. 'This was where my mother worshipped and where she sang.'

After that they ate out of his hand, though he did not use that expression.

Only once did I do business with him. I called on him in August 1957, on behalf of a group who were trying to negotiate the return to Ireland of the Lane pictures, a famous collection then in the possession of the National Gallery. There had been a prolonged dispute as to whether Sir Hugh Lane had bequeathed them to Ireland or to England.

On previous visits to Downing Street I had always been struck by the air, if not of tension, at least of great things afoot. This time the atmosphere was one of deliberate and profound relaxation. A courteous aide greeted me with the words: 'I am afraid the Prime Minister will be a few minutes late' (my appointment was at 10.30). 'He is having a long lie – a long lie,' he repeated, with smiling emphasis. This in fact was friendly play-acting; the Prime Minister kept me waiting about a minute, if as much. When I entered the Cabinet Room, and saw him sitting where Clem Attlee had sat so often, I was surprised to find that he treated me as a total stranger.

His tone at first astounded me. Not that it was personally offensive, but it was so completely blimpish. 'I gather', he said in effect, 'you want us to do something for the Irish. What have the Irish done for us? What did they do in the First World War? What, for that matter, did they do in the Second?' and he proceeded for a time like the most reactionary member of White's or the Turf Club. I was only too aware that my time was limited, presumably to half an hour, and that it was slipping away. I ventured to put it deferentially: 'You will hardly expect me, Prime Minister, to reply on the wider issue, but I have come about the Lane pictures. As you know, the Duke of Wellington has suggested that half the pictures might be sent to Ireland for, say, five years, and then the other half.'

His tone changed magically. In a moment he was the enlightened publisher, the forward-looking businessman. 'There might be something in that if it led to a settlement,' he said at once. And in a few minutes we had covered a great deal of practical ground to excellent purpose. He left me in no doubt, and wrote to tell me so afterwards in a letter which was not marked 'Confidential', that he himself favoured a solution on the lines suggested. But the Trustees of the National Gallery must be free to make up their own minds; the Government could use their good offices but could not coerce them. The deal went through, and the arrangement has endured.

Before I left his mood or tone changed for the second time. He had been the West End clubman; then the shrewd Scottish business type; now, for a few minutes, he became the visionary, almost the original crofter peering out through the western mists. What we had been discussing, even if it came off, was small stuff. Could it be a prelude to a much wider settlement? I reminded him of Cardinal d'Alton's interview that year under which an Indian solution would be offered to Ireland. She would remain a republic, but would be a member of the Commonwealth like India. The idea of Ireland returning to the Commonwealth stirred him visibly. 'I suppose such a thing has never happened before.' Nor does it show signs of happening now.

That anecdote brings out the three layers of his mind and temperament: the crofter grandfather, the true businessman, the West End clubman married to the daughter of a duke. To these should be added the devout child of Balliol and the lover of books and history. His sense of history has been paraded a shade too often. But of its authenticity there cannot be any doubt. We are told that he would always read for an hour before going to bed. Jane Austen, Dickens and Trollope are among his favourites, but he never loses contact with Thucydides. Ultimately I see him as more practical than academic. I cannot see him devoting his life to learning, though as Chancellor of Oxford University he has been superlative – beyond question the greatest Chancellor since the Duke of Wellington.

To say that Macmillan was an actor is true, but only a small part of the truth. He was many other things as well. The title of statesman cannot be denied him. Wilson wrote of him: 'Macmillan's role as a poseur was itself a pose.' The precise meaning of those words is unclear. There is no doubt, however, that once Macmillan reached his full stature in occupation of No. 10 Downing Street he discovered an act which was entirely natural and which gave widespread pleasure. Of all our eleven Prime Ministers he was the most complete all-rounder, equipped at all points in intellect and character, endowed above all with a supreme sense of direction and joy in managing his fellow-men.

Alec Douglas-Home

The Conservative Christian

DOUGLAS-HOME
Rt Hon. Sir Alexander Frederick
(1903–   )

M.P. (U) South Lanark, 1931–45;
(C) Lanark Division of Lanarkshire, 1950–1;
succeeded to title 14th Earl of Home in 1951
but disclaimed peerage, 23 October 1963;
M.P. (U) Kinross and West Perthshire, November 1963–September 1974.

Parliamentary Private Secretary to the Prime Minister, 1937–40;
Joint Parliamentary Under-Secretary, Foreign Office, May–July 1945;
Minister of State, Scottish Office, 1951–April 1955;
Secretary of State for Commonwealth Relations, 1955–60;
Deputy Leader of the House of Lords, 1956–7;
Leader of the House of Lords, and Lord President of the Council, 1957–60;
Secretary of State for Foreign Affairs, 1960–3;
Prime Minister and First Lord of the Treasury, October, 1963–4;
Leader of the Opposition, October 1964–July 1965;
Secretary of State for Foreign and Commonwealth Affairs, 1970–4.

K.T. 1962;
Created Baron Home of the Hirsel, 1974 (Life Peer).

The Conservative Christian

LORD HOME WAS Prime Minister for only a year – a shorter period than any other Prime Minister except Bonar Law, who died after eight months in office. Home's brief reign did not end in disaster like that of Anthony Eden after twenty months. He achieved a better result in the 1964 General Election than had been prophesied when he took over. In fact, he nearly won. His period of office, however, was not marked by anything notably good or bad, except that he left his successor a grave balance-of-payments deficit.

While still Foreign Secretary, and never expecting to reach the top position, he told a newspaper that he needed matches to work out sums. He admitted later that the remark was unfortunate. More seriously, his lack of experience in domestic Ministries apart from the Scottish Office handicapped him continuously. In this respect he resembled Eden. It is difficult to see how either of them could have overcome such a palpable disadvantage.

Seeking to give him his place in history, one is more interested in the man than in anything he achieved. After he was defeated at the General Election in 1964 he was soon displaced from the Conservative leadership. In his memoirs he describes the process calmly enough. He refers to the moves which were made to remove him from the leadership. 'All this', he says, 'was duly reported to me. My reaction was boredom with the whole business . . . I was grateful and touched by the many friends who urged me to fight. But I had no stomach for it. . . .' He was at all times a tough combatant where causes were concerned, but one can possibly adapt to him a phrase of Woodrow Wilson's: 'He was too proud to fight for himself.' What followed, however, has placed him high in the national roll of honour. He served without hesitation under Edward Heath, the man who had supplanted him. At the time of writing he is probably the most respected figure in the public life of Britain.

Alec Douglas-Home, born in 1903, still slim and elegant today after passing the age of eighty, was the son of a great Scottish landowner. He made the famous retort to Harold Wilson, who referred to him disparagingly as the fourteenth Earl of Home. 'I suppose', he said, 'that he is the fourteenth Mr Wilson.' There is plenty of wit in the Home family.

One of his brothers, William, the successful playwright, was sent to prison for a year for refusing on humanitarian grounds to obey a military order. Another, Henry, the well-known broadcaster on birds (incidentally, my 'fag' at Eton) was given a month's sentence for a motoring offence. On arrival at the prison he was handed a telegram from his brother. 'Don't worry, the first month is always the worst.'

Alec Home is the quintessential Old Etonian. Whether one 'takes to' his public image depends on one's reaction to the Old Etonian ethos. When I myself was at Eton he was President of Pop, the elected élite of the school. He was a splendid all-round athlete, in my recollection – which may not be accurate here – captain of the Cricket Eleven. Although only two years younger, and very high in the school for my age, I would not have dared to speak to him unless he had spoken to me first. And I cannot remember that happening. All his life the boys and men who have known him well, and had plenty to pick from, have chosen him their leader. But he remains to those outside such circles an aloof aristocrat; to some, before he became Foreign Secretary, an effete Bertie Wooster, a supposed weakling; whereas in fact, like Lord Salisbury – another 'effete aristocrat' – he has a character like steel.

His wife Elizabeth, the highly intelligent daughter of his headmaster and mine, Dr Alington, introduced a powerful strain of idealism. Her father was the most inspiring preacher I have ever listened to. Her mother was a member of the Lyttelton family unsurpassed by few if any families in its contribution to British culture and statesmanship. Her step-uncle Edward Lyttelton, often referred to as saintly, was Attlee's headmaster at Haileybury during the Boer War. Himself a strong anti-imperialist, he refused to give the boys a half-holiday when Ladysmith was relieved. The whole school protested, whereupon Lyttelton caned the entire middle school, including Attlee. Not the small boys, they could hardly be held responsible; not the sixth form, that would have been bad for discipline.

By the time of the first great war he was headmaster of Eton, but his attitude to war had not changed. Much was forgiven to a Lyttelton who had been such a fine cricketer, but his Christian attitude to the Germans led to his premature withdrawal. When I was at Eton the rumour spread that his daughter Hester Alington, wife of the headmaster, had voted Labour at the election. This caused much dismay.

Elizabeth and I stayed with the Alingtons when Dr Alington had become Dean of Durham. I was introduced by them to the near-starving population of Bishop Auckland. I am still haunted by the paper-thin faces of the men and women. Such food as came their way was passed on to the children. Everyone, bitterly critical of the Government, was loud in praise of the Alington family.

At Oxford Home excelled once again in sport (although he did not get a Blue) and socially. In 'schools' he achieved a Third, the same level as Baldwin. But as in the case of Baldwin, no one supposed that here was a third-class man. Soon he was a Conservative member of Parliament and PPS to Neville Chamberlain. He was satirically referred to as having carried Chamberlain's umbrella at Munich. No doubt he would have distinguished himself in the war, but he was stricken with an appalling illness, tuberculosis of the spine, which confined him to bed for more than two years. (There is a strange comparison with Macmillan here.) There is no doubt that the boy who was not considered particularly intellectual at Eton had become, by the end of the war, a well-read man.

Absorbed as I was after the war with my life as a junior Minister, I did not think much about the activities of Alec Home. But with the return of the Conservatives he became Minister of State for Scotland 1951–5, by this time having become the Earl of Home. He was Secretary of State for Commonwealth Relations 1955–60 and Leader of the House of Lords from 1957 onward. 'Alec Home will do it beautifully,' said Lord Salisbury to me when he himself resigned the position. He was Foreign Secretary from 1960 till 1963, when he left the Lords to become Prime Minister. He never lifted a finger to promote the change in the 1963 Act which enabled members of the House of Lords to renounce their peerages.

'Watch Home,' said my great friend Henry Burrows, later Assistant Clerk of the House of Lords, when Alec first began to speak as a Minister of State in the Scottish Office. I ignored the advice. But how right Henry was! At the time of Suez Alec Home put up a better debating defence of the indefensible policy than anyone in either House. He laid all his emphasis on the one point in his case that could at least be plausibly argued: 'We stopped a war.' By getting the argument on to ground where some parity of debate was possible he deflected attention from the more profound enormities, and extricated his colleagues with some show of dignity.

When he was appointed Foreign Secretary in summer 1960 there was general ignorance in even the well-informed Press about his capacities. Yet he had already been Leader of the House of Lords for three years, and not infrequently in his speeches carried the whole

House with him – a rare feat indeed outside the field of mere generality or pious tributes. It is a curious truth that the Press have never felt equal to assessing personal reputations in the Lords as they would normally do in the Commons. They seem to be baffled by the unemotional air of the Lords' audience, and the mutual (sometimes ironical) courtesies.

If we regard him purely in terms of leadership of the House of Lords, Alec Home need fear no obvious comparison. He was less flexible and unexpected than Christopher Addison, though sharper and neater in phrase. Less intuitive than William Jowitt, and less deadly in pressing an argument, but possessed, like Lord Grey of Fallodon, of the peculiar power of adding the force of his own character to the strength of his case. Less prophetic a moralist, and far less intolerant, than Albert Alexander, but well equipped to represent the sentiment of the House of Lords in the expression of his Christian beliefs. Less majestic than Salisbury, less glorious in vocabulary than Hailsham, narrower in range of subject and less fiery than either, he replied to a debate on *his own topics* more effectively than any of them. He dealt with the arguments of his opponents tersely and yet faithfully in the terms in which they conceived them.

When a friend in the Foreign Office asked me what he would be like as Foreign Secretary I replied, 'He'll be anti-communist, and he'll write his own speeches.' I was not proved wrong. He is, like Salisbury, a Christian Conservative statesman – with the accent on all three attributes. I would not say that a sense of the future is his strong feature. But when he told me that my speech introducing the Wolfenden Report on homosexualism was a superb performance I glowed with pride – and not merely because he was once President of Pop. . . .

When he defended the Suez adventure the conditions were very favourable to him. The number of Labour peers was still very small. When I wound up that debate for the Opposition I announced with great *éclat* that 'everyone on these benches feels as strongly as I do'. I glanced round impressively and found that our benches were completely empty. At the time I attributed Home's air of conviction to the particular form of regimental loyalty which has always been a special strength of the Conservative Party. But since reading his memoirs I have had to revise that opinion.

He goes out of his way to publish an appendix in his memoirs in which the speech on Suez is quoted at length with evident pride. We must therefore take it very seriously in assessing his international values; that is, the moral values he applies to international affairs.

Earlier in the book he gives us an account of the whole Suez affair which makes one rub one's eyes with incredulity. He pulls no punches in blaming the Americans (and he is no sort of anti-American) for letting us down. As in the memoirs of Eden and Macmillan, there is no trace of any guilt over the shocking collusion of the British Government with the French and the Israelis which led to the war. Runing through everything is an overriding awareness of the Soviet menace. I share this to the full, but that in my eyes is no excuse for abandoning accepted rules of international morality. In the speech under discussion he says, 'I do not believe that it is possible to understand the action [taken by the British Government in regard to Suez] or indeed to explain it and the recent events in the Middle East unless one looks at them against the background of Russian foreign policy in promoting international Communism. . . .' Then, as he approaches his peroration, he cries triumphantly,

> This may be one of those turning-points where the free world will begin to live and to breathe again. For China has not become a Russian satellite; Eastern Europe, with incredible bravery, is breaking the grip of Russia upon it, and in the Middle East Russian policy has had a setback which may have lasting consequences. I greatly welcome this opportunity to exorcise international Communism which has been the curse of mankind.

Anti-Communism! Fine. But anti-Communism is not enough. Alike from the point of view of statecraft and of morality, Conservatives today are inclined to say that our Suez aggression (though they don't refer to it as that) was all right in its idea, faulty only in its execution. I would submit on the contrary that no manœuvres and acts of force so contrary to our best traditions could ever have won the approval of the world, including most importantly the Commonwealth and the United States. The bungling of the operation was inherent in the immorality of the plan.

And here I must be allowed to pause. The Suez escapade was defended not only at the time but afterwards by three much respected British Prime Ministers, Eden, Macmillan and Home. Macmillan and Home were recognizably Christian, Home devoutly so. I am asserting that the policy they pursued at Suez was immoral, but certainly not that they were immoral men. We are driven back, it seems to me, on the distinction drawn by the famous American theologian Niebuhr, between moral man and immoral society.

Harold Nicolson in his account of the events leading up to the war of 1914 describes only two leaders involved as being morally unassailable: Edward Grey, the British Foreign Secretary, and

Bethmann-Hollwegg, the German Chancellor. Yet no two men could have been so utterly opposed in their policies or later in their understanding of the causes of the war. It was Bethmann-Hollwegg who referred to the promise to preserve Belgian neutrality as a scrap of paper. He began his crucial speech to the Reichstag: 'Gentlemen, we are in a state of necessity and necessity knows no law.'

At the Versailles Peace Conference the Allies forced the Germans to sign a treaty acknowledging their entire responsibility for the war. By the time I was teaching international relations professionally at Oxford there was a general agreement that the blame should be widely spread. I am certainly not saying that there is no such thing as international morality. I am saying that the differences of opinion will always be far more pronounced than those in regard to personal conduct.

Whether it would or would not have been wrong to seek to overthrow Nasser by force after he had nationalized the Suez Canal can be argued. I myself will always believe that it would have been wrong, but I can recognize another point of view. Once a defiance of the United Nations was involved the moral case for intervention became still weaker. But the collusion with the French and Israeli governments to produce a hypocritical case for intervention will, I feel sure, stand condemned for all time. The eminent Prime Ministers mentioned above have found discretion the better of valour in dealing with it in their memoirs.

Alec Home is a true patriot, shrewd and tenacious, but he has at no time appeared to understand the rationality of the hopes which have animated so many in this country and abroad that one day a better system of international peace-keeping will be established. It is not easy reading his published works to say just how far he justifies today Neville Chamberlain's policy of appeasement. He has much that is most interesting to say about that policy in his *Letters to a Grandson*. But it is clear from that book that he remains sceptical about the possibilities for peace that were contained in the concept of the League of Nations, and that have resided, since the war, in the United Nations.

In *Letters to a Grandson* he asks the question: If blame is to be allocated on the Western side, where should it lie? He provides a ten-point answer, in the course of which our failure to rearm much more rapidly is duly stressed. His first two points are these: We must blame 1) The slogan adopted after the 1914–18 war that this had been the 'war to end all wars', which derived from the horror of the experience, rather than a sober strategic calculation of dangers present and impending. 2) The depth of the British people's conviction that the League of Nations would provide a substitute for national defence.

I shall go to my grave believing that if the League of Nations had been properly supported between the wars we could have indeed prevented the great catastrophe that followed. But it needed more faith and hope than the Conservative leaders in this country could find room for in their philosophy.

That is not to deny that Home, Foreign Secretary again from 1970 to 1974, exhibited not only moral but high technical qualities in that role. There is much to be learnt from his writings, particularly the letters to his grandson, as to how the West should handle their affairs with the Soviet Union, peacefully but resolutely. He writes,

> I hope that I have been able to illustrate to you the horrible choice which constantly faces the democracies. Our instincts are all for the quiet life, so that we may concentrate the benefits of scientific development on the betterment of the lives of men and women. Massive sums spent annually on rearmament clearly frustrate this purpose, but what alternative have we if the Russians insist on forcing the pace in the interest of a Communist take-over?'

The type of approach he recommends is best illustrated, he writes, by advice given by Dr Jowett, the Master of Balliol. ' "Don't expect too much," he once said to a young man, and "don't attempt too little." That almost exactly represents my approach to disarmament negotiations', says Home, 'with the Soviet Union. The recipe', he says, 'is to combine prudence, not expecting too much, with initiatives not attempting too little. My forecast is that you and yours will survive.' In general terms, one can hardly improve on that guidance. Always there is the underlying assumption that we will maintain our strength, but, in accordance with our Christian religion, make sure that there is always restraint in our use of power.

Of our eleven Prime Ministers the majority have been recognized Christians. All of them have subscribed to Christian ethics. None of them has spoken out so clearly and unequivocally about his Christian beliefs as Alec Home, although statesmen just below the rank of Prime Minister have done likewise. George Lansbury, Lord Halifax, Stafford Cripps and Lord Hailsham are four who come to mind. In his memoirs, Home quotes an earlier speech of his own which includes the passage: 'The existence of a Lord of creation working through the minds of men answers much of the persistent craving in the hearts of the human race, but of course we look for more. We look for the whole truth.' He goes on to add: 'I am not sure that, in the absence of the complete truth, I do ask for very much more; for if it is a fact (and Dr Alington convinced me that it is) that Christ was God's personal messenger to man, then the gap which has to be bridged by faith is much less daunting.'

What other Prime Minister since Gladstone could have spoken in words like those? Alec Home drew, no doubt, profound inspiration from Cyril Alington, his old headmaster and mine, and his father-in-law. So did I from a little further off. He ends the chapter quoted from with the characteristically modest yet indomitable assertion: 'I just and only just dare to say I believe.' The reason why he is so universally respected should by now be apparent.

When the Conservative leadership suddenly became vacant in 1963 the three most obvious candidates were R. A. Butler, Lord Hailsham and Reginald Maudling, all men of high repute who had obtained a First in Honour Moderations. But it was Home, whose degree was no better than a Third, who was the dark horse that 'came through on the rails' – a triumph of character. Those who had pinned their hopes on his character were not disappointed in his premiership or afterwards.

Harold Wilson

The Daring Pilot

WILSON
Rt Hon. Sir (James) Harold
(1916–   )

M.P. (Lab.) Huyton Division of Lancs. since 1950 (Ormskirk Division, 1945–50).

Director of Economics and Statistics, Ministry of Fuel and Power, 1943–4;
Parliamentary Secretary to Ministry of Works, 1945–March 1947;
Secretary for Overseas Trade, March–October 1947;
President, Board of Trade, October 1947–April 1951;
Chairman: Labour Party Executive Committee, 1961–2;
Public Accounts Committee, 1959–63;
Leader, Labour Party, 1963–76;
Prime Minister and First Lord of the Treasury, 1964–70, 1974–6;
Leader of the Opposition, 1963–4, 1970–4.

K.G. 1976;
Created Baron of Rievaulx, 1983.

The Daring Pilot

OCTOBER 1964. Here I was, back in the long Cabinet Room at No. 10 Downing Street where I had so often called on Clem Attlee, then Prime Minister, and, though not a member of the Cabinet, attended not a few of its meetings. I had entered that room once only in the thirteen 'wasted years' of Conservative rule. But now my host was Harold Wilson, far more euphoric than Clem Attlee ever allowed himself to appear.

'I want you to be Leader of the House of Lords,' he began. I matched his euphoria with my own. 'You'll be Lord Privy Seal, and of course a member of the Cabinet. It ought to be Lord President of the Council, but they told me that that post had to be in the Commons.' (To this day I cannot imagine who could have given him this obviously erroneous advice.)

He mentioned a senior Labour peer who felt entitled to the position of Leader of the Lords, adding: 'But I asked Clem Attlee. He said, "It must be Frank Pakenham."' (I had been Longford for over three years.) This was no time for quibbling. Harold Wilson concluded our little discussion with the words: 'We'll have a lot of fun together.' And so for a long time we did.

Of all the Prime Ministers in the present century Harold Wilson is the only one who came to an end of his own volition. Baldwin would come nearest to him in this respect. But Baldwin, we are told, had a nervous breakdown before his last year in office and another one at the end of it. He must therefore be reckoned one of the six Prime Ministers who retired because of advancing years or ill health or both. The others were Salisbury, Bonar Law (who died in office), Eden (who collapsed), Churchill and Macmillan. Four others were forced to resign without a general election: Balfour, Asquith, Lloyd George and Chamberlain. Four more (including the last three) resigned from the premiership or the leadership immediately or soon after an electoral defeat of their party: Attlee, Home, Heath and Callaghan.

Wilson was no more than sixty when he took the world by surprise by announcing his intended resignation. There were plentiful speculations as to the reasons behind his decision. Sinister explanations were produced for which there was no evidence whatever, then or later. The true explanation was undoubtedly that which he gave at the time. After thirteen years' leadership of the Labour Party (a longer period than anyone except Attlee with twenty years), after winning four general elections out of five, after eight years as Prime Minister, a longer period than any Prime Minister in peace-time in this century, he had had enough. He had surely earned his retirement.

He did not receive the accolade that might reasonably have been expected. He continued for seven years as a member of the House of Commons, but neither made nor attempted to make much of a mark there. He differed here from his successor James Callaghan, who continued to deliver weighty speeches. On the other hand, Wilson did not undergo the experience of Callaghan of being booed at a Labour Party Conference.

Harold Wilson remained immensely popular in his constituency of Huyton. When he arrived in the House of Lords, where I had the honour to be one of his sponsors, he was at once accepted with pleasure, and has since then made an admirable impression. He became a Knight of the Garter, in the personal gift of the Queen, the first Prime Minister to be so honoured during my time as a member of that order (thirteen years). Nothing could be a clearer refutation of the unspecified sneers which were cooked up against him when he gave up the leadership.

Edward Heath and Harold Wilson are alike in failing to exert influence at home after leaving No. 10 (Heath has had considerable influence abroad). But the cases are in no way identical. When Heath was evicted from the leadership of the Conservative Party, and Mrs Thatcher installed in his place, he was left with a deep and understandable sense of bitterness which unwisely he made no attempt to conceal. Since 1976 Wilson has never done or said anything which should have embarrassed his successors or the Labour Party. He has been at all times careful and frequently generous. The reasons for his absence of legitimate influence must be sought elsewhere.

First and foremost one should mention his health. I know no more of Harold Wilson's medical life than does the average newspaper reader. But everyone is aware that he has undergone at least one serious operation and he was in a weak state of health for some time afterwards. It may well be that even without the medical factor he would not have wished to play a dominant part as an elder statesman. As things were it was out of the question.

Nevertheless, health apart, few writers have come forward to say much that is favourable about the Wilson years. Dick Crossman and

Barbara Castle were probably closer to him than any two other members of the Cabinet when he formed his administration in 1964. Their absorbing diaries need not be taken literally. They give an impression of Harold Wilson which does not leave a happy taste in the mouth.

One may ask if anyone comes out of these diaries much better than Harold Wilson. The answer to that is 'No'. Nevertheless, these diaries leave an all too clear impression of Wilson the Machiavellian man. In something I wrote twenty years ago on Harold Wilson I spent some time discussing and refuting the charge of 'deviousness'. I would say the same today but I realize more clearly than I did then why this charge was levelled against him in the first place, and stuck to him for many years.

No one can question his great intellectual capacity. When he got his First in the Honours School of Philosophy, Politics and Economics at Oxford his marks were said to be the best since that school was founded. No Prime Minister since Asquith has had such good results in the Schools. One cannot say how he would have fared in a cultural or purely scientific subject. But no one, I would submit, has ever entered politics with a more effective mental equipment. He has always possessed an immense power of rapid assimilation, a splendid memory (not quite as perfect as he supposes), powers of dissection and analysis equalled by those of exposition. God has further given him a fertile wit and an unforced sense of humour. When I add great powers of work, plenty of physical and mental stamina, and much ambition, we are presented with a man who one would think would be bound to get to the top. Which is precisely where he got to, and where for a long time he stayed.

Did an evil fairy manage to insert some defect of character to counteract these great advantages? Fundamentally, no. One cannot begin to assess him accurately until one realizes that he is a very nice, in particular a very kind man. Much of the idealism that he acquired as an active Boy Scout has stayed with him and will stay with him to the end.

My wife has recently been looking up some letters that I wrote to her during the Wilson years. (I never ventured to copy Asquith and scribble them during Cabinet meetings.) I often commented on this 'kindness' of Harold Wilson's. When Frank Soskice's health made his retirement from the Cabinet inevitable Harold Wilson took enormous trouble to find him alternative occupation. Rather to my surprise, I report myself as sometimes the only member of the Cabinet who enjoyed all his jokes – a reference, for example, to a

Cabinet meeting at Chequers as the best sort of open prison 'once you send their cars away'.

I will give one example of his kindness which cannot possibly be attributed to the general search for popularity attributed to politicians. While he was a very preoccupied Prime Minister he found time to come to the wedding of my daughter Rachel. He was introduced to a large company of guests, including my former secretary, Mrs Motteram (by then an octogenarian, and totally blind). An hour or so later he took his leave, but before going insisted on searching out Mrs Motteram. 'I can't go without saying goodbye to Mrs Motteram', whom of course he had never heard of until then. He got pleasure and he gave pleasure by going out of his way to do a kindly thing.

A little scene at a Labour peers' reception soon after he entered the House is also characteristic. He and Hugh Gaitskell had disagreed about many things, and to put it bluntly, had been rivals. Nevertheless, on the occasion I have in mind I came across him and Dora Gaitskell in affectionate conversation. Dora said to me as I approached, 'Harold saved my life by nominating me for a life peerage when Hugh died.' Harold had told me earlier when I became leader of the party, 'The first thing I decided to do was to nominate Dora for a life peerage.' So now these two old adversaries were locked in a happy friendship.

The more, however, that I reflect on his period of pre-eminence, the more I think of him as a beleaguered spirit, a man who rightly or wrongly felt always that he had to get up very early in the morning to survive. He was often accused of having a conspiracy complex, and the criticism was not without truth. I repeat at this point that he was an extremely good chairman of the Cabinet, different from Attlee, much more genial but no less effective. His loquacity, an old weakness of his, was kept under stern control.

Yet even in that area there was one palpable weakness. The modern non-attributable use of the parliamentary lobby places a peculiar temptation in the way of a Prime Minister, to whom the lobby look for special guidance. I have heard Harold Wilson talk of 'roughing up' a Conservative opponent 'on lobby terms'. I remember that on one occasion he told me that a Cabinet colleague was briefing the Press against him. Soon afterwards a Cabinet colleague told me that the Prime Minister was briefing the Press against *him*.

Harold Wilson used often to complain of leaks from his Cabinet, but he was regarded by many of us as being responsible for the atmosphere that produced them. Such things would have been impossible in the days of Clement Attlee, who was almost too restrictive in his attitude to the Press. I was, however, intrigued to read in

Penny Junor's *Life of Mrs Thatcher* that those around her considered that no Prime Minister had ever suffered as much as she had from leakages.

When Wilson formed his Cabinet in 1964 he was the youngest Prime Minister during the present century. He made no secret of his desire to lower the average age, which was not encouraging to some of his older colleagues. For example, I was always referred to in the Press as Longford (59) or later as Longford (60) or Longford (61). Sources close to Wilson such as Dick Crossman and George Wigg forecast my early exclusion. A journalist once showed me a transcript of a press conference in which Wilson was asked about possible Cabinet changes and replied that there had been a good deal of speculation about the future of the Leader of the House of Lords (that was me). He said he did not wish to comment on that matter at the moment, but the implication was clear enough.

I am making two points here: (1) He talked too freely to the Press; (2) He talked too freely to everyone, partly out of sheer friendliness, partly out of a subconscious desire to impress. Lord Shackleton, Deputy Leader of the Lords, six years younger than me, would obviously be succeeding me in due course. We agreed afterwards that Harold Wilson had given different impressions to him and me as to when that was likely to occur. It was this kind of thing which damaged Harold's reputation even among those who, like Eddie Shackleton and me, were very fond of him and admired him.

The development of his career undoubtedly affected his approach to life and politics. Harold Wilson was born in 1916, the son of James Herbert and Ethel Wilson of Huddersfield. His father was an industrial chemist, sometimes out of work. Harold attended Milnsbridge Council School and Royds Hall School, Huddersfield. He made his way to the Wirral Grammar School, Bevington, Cheshire, and thence to Jesus College, Oxford. There he not only obtained an outstanding First in Philosophy, Politics and Economics but won the Gladstone Memorial Prize for History, and the Webb Medley Economics scholarship. In those days he was a Liberal – suspicious, it may be, of an undergraduate Labour Party, which was strongly tainted with communism. He became a lecturer in economics at New College and then a Fellow of University College, just before the war.

During the war he became Director of Economics and Statistics at the Ministry of Fuel and Power.

In 1945 he was elected to Parliament as a Labour MP at the age of twenty-nine, and immediately made a junior Minister. (So was I, ten years older, in the Lords.) Within two years, still only thirty-one, he entered the Cabinet as President of the Board of Trade, far ahead of his contemporaries. Wilson, the young Research Fellow of University College, Oxford, Attlee's beloved college, was brought forward rapidly by Attlee and Cripps, who became the economic supremo. His rival as it proved was a protégé of Hugh Dalton: Hugh Gaitskell, a man of destiny cut off later in his prime. The so-called Hampstead Set centring round Hugh Gaitskell were a generation older than Wilson. No doubt he was made to feel an outsider, by them and by their own protégés, even younger than Wilson, like Roy Jenkins and Tony Crosland. Whoever might be supposed to belong to that circle, Wilson evidently did not.

These circumstances placed him to the left of the Labour Party, where he did not naturally belong. He resigned from the Cabinet with Aneurin Bevan in 1951, referred to unpleasantly by Hugh Dalton as 'Nye's little dog'. He is still entitled to argue that the military expenditure he was objecting to was more than our economy could stand. But he was never a real Bevanite. He was out of place in that *galère*. It was unfortunate that his career depended on his emergence as one of their standard-bearers.

Wilson has always been a patriot. The phrase can be applied to any public-spirited politician, left or right, but it has a considerable significance in regard to Wilson. Men like Churchill and Macmillan, patriots by any standard, had a lot of time for Wilson. So did Lord Home, who gave Harold Wilson much pleasure by coming to a lunch given by my friend Lord Kagan to welcome him to the House of Lords. We are told by Nigel Fisher, biographer of Macmillan, that Macmillan did not like Gaitskell and did like Wilson. This was in spite of the fact that Wilson had not fought in the war, though he was still in his early twenties when it broke out. (He had volunteered for active service but was directed into statistical work.) Wilson tells various stories of Churchill in an illuminating essay in *A Prime Minister on Prime Ministers*.

The one I like best relates to Churchill's attitude when Wilson, along with Aneurin Bevan, resigned from the Attlee Cabinet (1951). Brendan Bracken approached Wilson on behalf of 'the greatest living statesman' (in other words, Winston Churchill), who wished Wilson to convey a message to his wife Mary.

> Churchill [writes Wilson] wanted me to know he had been 'presented' to my wife, otherwise he would not presume to send her a message. The message was that whereas I, as an experienced politician, had taken a step of which he felt free to take such party advantage as was appropriate, his concern was with my wife, an innocent party in these affairs, who would undoubtedly suffer in consequence; he recalled the number of occasions his wife had suffered as a result of his own political decisions.

Would I therefore convey to her his personal sympathy and understanding?

Wilson delivered the messsage to his wife. It was greeted with gratitude and tears. Next day he saw Churchill in the smoke-room and conveyed the thanks of his wife. Immediately, tears flooded down the face of the elderly statesman. Harold Wilson recounted the interview to Mary. Once again, she burst into tears. Wilson comments, whimsically: 'Two days earlier I had been a minister of the Crown, red box and all; now I was reduced to the position of a messenger between my wife and Winston Churchill, each of whom burst into tears on receipt of a message from the other.'

There is no doubt that the old statesman was fond of the young one. Wilson had antagonized most of the Tories by his hard-hitting polemics at their expense. But Churchill and Macmillan could laugh that sort of thing off and discern the patriot beneath the party trumpeter. No one who has read Wilson's glowing tributes to Churchill could doubt that on his part there was an enormous admiration for the man who saved the country.

Yet if I had had a vote (which as a peer I did not have), I would have voted for Brown or possibly Callaghan rather than Wilson in the leadership election of 1963. I would have assumed that Harold Wilson, like others on the left of the party, was unsound on the Atlantic Alliance.

The death of Hugh Gaitskell was a tragic event not only for his many personal friends – we had shared rooms in our last year at Oxford – but also for large numbers of uncommitted people who regarded him as the embodiment of principle in politics. Anyone who sees an old film of him speaking about Suez will feel that something went out of British politics with his death and never returned. If he cared about one issue more than another, apart from his long-standing devotion to human equality, it was the American alliance. Was all that to go for nothing now? Not at all, as it turned out.

In fact as soon as Harold became leader he retained Patrick Gordon Walker, a deeply committed atlanticist, as the Shadow Foreign Secretary, and assured him that he would be the Foreign Secretary if Labour came into power. He was even better than his word. He appointed Gordon Walker as Foreign Secretary even though he was defeated in the General Election at Smethwick, and only let him go with reluctance when he was later defeated in a by-election at Leyton. As I see it, Wilson abandoned his left-wing approach to foreign policy as soon as he became leader of the party in favour of one much more adapted to his true instincts. All through his time in office he pursued a foreign policy towards America which was not distinguishable from the one that would have been pursued by Hugh Gaitskell.

Speaking broadly, the same could be said of the domestic policy of the Wilson government, 1964–70. From 1974 to 1976 there was a derogation, admittedly. Michael Foot was brought in as Minister of Employment with the obvious purpose of satisfying the trade unions. This he did beyond question, but in my eyes the process was carried much too far, with disastrous consequences. When Wilson ceased to be Prime Minister in 1976 he had in terms of popularity got the worst of all worlds. He had incurred the wrath of the Tories by his devastating attacks on them. He had never won the final confidence of the right wing of the Labour Party because he had for so long been identified with the left, but the left had never felt that he was quite one of them. The policies of his government had confirmed this suspicion. The general public had nevertheless retained a warm spot for him.

His final Honours List did him further damage. The gut reaction to it was unfavourable, though, as I see it, unfair. I was privileged to introduce two of the new peers. The list contained more interesting names than usual, but there seemed to be little connection between some of them and Labour politics. Suspicions were freely expressed that personal considerations played too large a part. The hubbub took a long time to die down.

When a small boy he was taken by his father to stand and be photographed on the doorstep of No. 10 Downing Street and was told that that was where he should one day finish. I have long thought that this duty to succeed imposed itself too early and heavily on Harold Wilson. I speculate that his evident desire to impress, to win every argument and to get the best of every deal is linked with the fear of falling below the standard set for him in early life.

He has been accused, not without reason, of a tendency to boastfulness, but his alleged boasting is in no way a sign of conceit or arrogance. It springs from an inner need to reassure himself that he really has fulfilled his father's highest expectations. Could not the same be said of a great man like Lord Mountbatten, who had the same small weakness?

What of his ultimate services to Britain and to humanity? I mention humanity because Harold Wilson has never been a narrow nationalist, as anyone will be aware who has read his early book, *War on Want*. Here one's conclusions will be much affected by one's political values. Indubitably he held the Labour Party together for thirteen years, as no other contemporary could have done. What Hugh Gaitskell might or might not have achieved if he had lived is beyond calculation. If we believe in the superiority of Labour ideas, or even in the contribution to the nation of an effective Opposition, we must give Wilson much credit here.

Some surprise was felt that Harold Wilson, when elected Leader of the Party in 1963, so quickly unified it, after the long struggles of the 1950s, or, as some would put it, completed so rapidly the unifying work of Hugh Gaitskell. There was no surprise in this for me at all. Harold Wilson, as I wrote at the time, was naturally a unifying influence on the Labour Party, just as Clem Attlee was – and for the same reason. His whole thought and character had been built up in their maturity within the Labour Party framework, in spite of a short Liberal phase at Oxford. The same was true of Clem Attlee. Though Attlee's family was anything but socialist, he had become an ardent socialist by his middle twenties. Just like Clem Attlee, Harold Wilson was part of the Labour movement, indistinguishable from it in a way that is true of few socialist intellectuals, however dedicated. Without conscious effort, Harold Wilson throughout most of his career has found himself sharing the feelings of the typical party man. That might not be quite so true after serving for some years as Prime Minister. But a Prime Minister can hardly be said to be typical of any section of society, even of the small group of Prime Ministers.

By any standards his action in standing against Hugh Gaitskell for the leadership in 1960 can be seen in retrospect to have been unwise. It created – or at least enhanced – unnecessary antagonisms; it gave a false impression of his personality. But he honestly believed that the party was being unnecessarily divided, and this, coupled with his dependence on the Left for his own support, led him into steps which were out of character.

When he became leader he recovered, with one or two masterly strokes, his true position in the middle. He has the talents of a natural unifier. He has a quick, shrewd and sympathetic grasp of what anyone he meets is after. As Gladstone said of Joseph Chamberlain, he is a good man to talk business to.

Did Britain under Wilson make more economic progress than in similar periods under the Conservatives? As has been pointed out by Professor Meade, for example, for twenty-five years after the war – that is, up to 1970 – 'the standard of living grew more rapidly than at any time in our history, though we were often apt to regard it as a period of failure because we were not growing as rapidly as the majority of other similar economies'. In that perspective the earlier Wilson years (1964–70) were no better and no worse than those which preceded them. In 1973 came the oil crisis, and for that and other reasons a period of international difficulty. The later Wilson years (1974–6) emerged quite well in comparison with those that followed. Both in the earlier and the later period there was a failure on the part of the Labour Government, as of all other post-war governments, to find a solution to the problem of curbing inflation without mass unemployment.

By the time I resigned from the Wilson Cabinet the shadow of a confrontation with the trades unions was already looming up. The remorseless pressure of wage demands was already beginning to threaten any national planning. Barbara Castle warned us, I recall, that we could either have a political crisis now or an economic crisis later. We tacitly opted for the latter.

After my departure the issue became more and more acute. I shall always think that Barbara Castle was on the right lines when, as Secretary of State for Employment and Productivity, she produced her paper *In Place of Strife*, to cope with strikes, particularly unofficial strikes. Harold Wilson went up to and beyond the line of duty in backing her. He knew well what ought to be done, but his Cabinet colleagues were faint-hearted, and he had to give way to them. Strictly speaking, there was no direct connection between *In Place of Strife* and an incomes policy. But the defeat under the first head made it still less likely that there would be success under the second.

At once Harold Wilson was putting a bright face on the turn-about. Too bright a face, one might think, for his ultimate credibility. But his optimism, his buoyancy, his resilience are closely linked with his underlying fortitude, which has indeed proved serviceable to himself and the country.

It would be agreeable to think that in our Government of 1964–7 we had done something to expand the social services more rapidly and to distribute wealth more fairly than any Tory Government in similar circumstances. On these points there has been much controversy since that time. Roy Jenkins, Chancellor of the Exchequer for the last half of the period, provides as good a perspective as anyone. Jenkins insisted that the Wilson Government had much to be proud of in its social record; but that we certainly could have done better and certainly must do better next time.

Jenkins recognized the persistent trouble with the balance of payments, and partly due to that our failure to achieve economic growth. On the first point, no one is better qualified to speak. We inherited a large balance-of-payments deficit, and after two and a half years of Jenkins as Chancellor of the Exchequer we emerged with a substantial surplus. Unemployment, however, had for the first time by 1970 passed the million mark.

Certainly we were bedevilled at all times by the fear of a run on the pound. At the end of our very first Cabinet meeting (October 1964) Jim Callaghan, Chancellor of the Exchequer, sent us home happy by announcing, 'I have just heard that the pound has had a good day.' Throughout the six years the pound sometimes had a good day, sometimes a bad one; good or bad, its shadow fell across us at all times.

For a long while Harold Wilson was inclined to identify the value of the pound with prestige, the prestige of the country, of the Labour Government and himself. Before the first Cabinet ever met he had decided with Callaghan and Brown (Chancellor of the Exchequer and Secretary of State for Economic Affairs respectively) that sterling must not be devalued. He was still insisting on that position and holding off strong Cabinet opposition to it in 1966. Not until 1967 was he forced to give way. It is easy to say that he was too rigid for the first three years of his government in this respect. It hardly becomes me to say so loudly, as I supported him at the time.

A socialist expert I respect has argued that, in our attempts to redistribute wealth, 'we were running up a descending escalator'. In other words, the natural bias of a market economy (even a mixed one like ours) would if left to itself promote increased inequality. This conclusion would fit in with the argument of Roy Jenkins (before he left the Labour Party) that a future Labour Government if true to its principles must set out to reverse such a trend much more deliberately and systematically. With which I cannot fail to agree.

I shall be reminded at this point that I resigned from the Wilson Cabinet of 1968. How far does that fact involve an adverse judgment on their social policies? I resigned exclusively because, under the impact of yet another financial crisis, it was decided to postpone the raising of the school-leaving age. In my letter of resignation I wrote:

> The postponement is apparently condemned by those educationalists whose opinion I value most. It is sharply opposed to the long-term policy and fundamental ideals of our party and the pledges we gave as recently as last September. It is inconceivable that I should commend it to the House of Lords.

In my resignation speech in the House of Lords I made it plain that I wished nothing but good to the Wilson Government. I deliberately kept the issue as narrow as possible. But on a deeper level I was shocked that we were being repeatedly told that, owing to the financial crisis, there must be 'no sacred cows'. In other words, there seemed to me an unlimited prospect of forsaking commitments. Looking back, I recall what Lord Salisbury wrote to me at the time. He wrote, as he himself said, from 'some small experience of resignation'. In fact, he was the only politician living to have resigned from two governments (Chamberlain's, 1938, and Macmillan's, 1957). 'People will always say', he wrote, 'that it is the wrong time and the wrong issue. It will never be the right time and the right issue. But when you reach the point when you know in your heart that it is impossible for you not to resign, then, if you do resign, you will never regret it.'

Writing some ten years ago – that is to say, six years after these events – I summed up my complaint against the Wilson Government in the phrase 'a shortage of radical passion'.

> It was not [I wrote] that the Labour Cabinet lacked sincerity in their desire to help the poor or under-privileged in this country, or the under-developed people overseas. But they lacked any fire in their belly remotely comparable to that of – shall we say – Lloyd George (by no means my hero) in his Radical days; or of some of Attlee's Cabinet.

Writing today, I do not see the problem in quite that way. Looking back now, it seems to me that the spirit was willing, but the intellectual guidelines were lacking. The socialist vision had provided not only the moral but the intellectual basis for the great reforms of 1945–51. From 1964–70, we were consulting the sacred books and finding them more like the Delphic oracles. For this it would be totally unfair to blame Harold Wilson personally. If he had come to power in 1945 (at the appropriate age) he might have made a great Prime Minister.

On the international side, I shall always applaud the firmness of our adherence to the Atlantic Pact and to our special relationship with the United States. I shall be sorry that we took so long to apply for entry to the Common Market and glad that we reached the right decision in the end, though our application was not at that time successful. In the same way, I am glad that we took the plunge and eventually extricated ourselves from most of our commitments east of Suez. Harold Wilson told me after meeting President Johnson for the first time that he got on with him very well – 'But I couldn't help wondering what would happen if he began to go round the bend. If I began to go round the bend, there would always be the Cabinet to stop me.' I said, 'What about Anthony Eden and Suez?' 'Ah,' he replied cryptically, 'I am not Anthony Eden.'

I have much respect for Harold Wilson's intelligence, courage and human kindness. His political skills can be illustrated by the fact that he won four out of five general elections. No one else in our century has won more than two. Gladstone can also be credited, a little doubtfully, with four victories – in 1868, 1880, 1885 and 1892. Harold Wilson, if anyone of our time, can be described as a master of the art of politics. If in many eyes there remains some uncertainty as to what he stood for, there was no doubt in the mind of the person whose opinion he would value most – the Queen. He is the only living Knight of the Garter who was appointed while still a member of the House of Commons. To adapt the words of Catherine of Aragon, 'He could wish no other herald.'

Edward Heath

The European

HEATH
Rt Hon. Edward Richard George
(1916–   )

M.P. (C) Bexley, Sidcup, since 1974 (Bexley, 1950–74).

Assistant Conservative Whip, February 1951;
Lord Commissioner of the Treasury, November 1951,
and Joint Deputy Government Chief Whip, 1952,
and Deputy Government Chief Whip, 1953–5
Parliamentary Secretary to the Treasury, and Government Chief Whip,
December 1955–October 1959;
Minister of Labour, October 1959–July 1960;
Lord Privy Seal, with Foreign Office responsibilities, 1960–3;
Secretary of State for Industry, Trade, Regional Development
and President of the Board of Trade, October 1963–October 1964;
Leader of the Opposition, 1965–70;
Prime Minister and First Lord of the Treasury, 1970–4;
Leader of the Opposition, 1974–5.

The European

'TED IS A BIG MAN, a world statesman,' said a former member of his Cabinet. This was in summer 1981, six years after Ted Heath had been removed from the Conservative leadership in favour of Margaret Thatcher, more than two years after the election victory which had made her Prime Minister. By that date (1981) Ted Heath had forfeited much goodwill in the House of Commons for refusing to treat Mrs Thatcher as one would normally treat one's elected leader. However, at that time the popularity of Mrs Thatcher herself was at a low ebb. My well-informed friend was convinced that a partnership between Prime Minister Mrs Thatcher and Chancellor of the Exchequer Ted Heath was the one clue to recovery. Most people today would say that such a project was 'never on'; but it is worth recalling that in 1981 it still seemed possible.

I have never known Ted Heath really well, but I have always enjoyed friendly relations with him since he was a young Conservative at Oxford and I was a somewhat older socialist don. He at Balliol – I at Christ Church. Like another Balliol man of an earlier vintage, Harold Macmillan, he set aside his Conservative allegiance to support A. D. Lindsay, Master of Balliol, in the by-election at Oxford which occurred just after Munich. As mentioned elsewhere, I was in Lindsay's corner throughout. Ted Heath, then as always at once ambitious and high-principled, was ready to risk his career on a moral issue. Shortly afterwards he was elected President of the Union on a Conservative anti-Chamberlain ticket. On one occasion he proposed the motion that 'this House has no confidence in the Chamberlain government as at present constituted'. That Government, it proclaimed, was neither more nor less than an organized hypocrisy, composed of Conservatives with nothing to conserve and Liberals with a hatred of liberty.

Thirty years later I was writing to him on behalf of the firm of publishers Sidgwick & Jackson, of which I was then chairman. I asked whether he would do a book for us on sailing. He wrote not only that book but two more for us – one on music, one on travel. All three were immensely successful. The travel book was no doubt such as other politicians might have produced. But no Prime Minister at any time could have written books remotely resembling *Sailing* and *Music*. Indeed, with the exception of Churchill who wrote a popular book on painting, none of our select eleven has written any book outside the field of politics past or present. Balfour, Prime Minister 1902–5, comes to mind for his writing and lectures on philosophy. Gladstone wrote on Homer and various aspects of religion. Disraeli's novels are still read quite widely. The list is not long.

Ted Heath wrote the books on sailing and music quickly. They were the outcome of a profound interest in both subjects. In the case of music it was life-long. His serious concern with sailing did not begin until 1966, yet by 1969 he had won one of the world's toughest ocean races – Sydney to Hobart. In 1971 he was captain of Britain, and won the Admiral's Cup. He tells us that he originally took up sailing in the interests of his health. 'I had music as a recreation, concert-going, opera, piano-playing, conducting a concert once a year and listening to stereo, but that was a spiritual experience. I had nothing physical except swimming.' His musical feats are too numerous to mention. Perhaps the most notable occurred on 25 November 1971, when he conducted the London Symphony Orchestra in Elgar's *Cockaigne Overture*. What other Prime Minister could point to a remotely similar performance outside his official duties? Lord Rosebery won the Derby twice while Prime Minister, but his personal responsibility for the victories must be regarded as minimal.

I was once sitting near the front when Ted Heath was again conducting the London Philharmonic Orchestra. He was instantly and magically transformed. It was as though he was all of a sudden fulfilled. For me, knowing him only in social and political life, it was a revelation. It appears that Prince Albert went through a similar transformation and fulfilment when engaged in playing the organ.

We can argue to the end of time what makes a complete man. There will be many to say that Heath, by remaining a bachelor, deprives himself automatically of the title. And certainly he would surely find it easier to enter into the minds of ordinary people if he had become a family man. But no one seeing him as I did on the occasion mentioned could fail to realize that on one plane of feeling he is more complete than any of his political contemporaries. It is worth recalling, perhaps, that A. J. Balfour, the only bachelor Prime Minister since the Younger Pitt at the end of the eighteenth century, was said to find his greatest happiness in music.

Yet at the time of writing this gifted, upright and determined man is an isolated political figure. Robert Behrens published in 1980 a monograph on the Conservative Party from Heath to Thatcher. In his final assessment he writes: 'There is some consolation for Mr Heath in the fact that at a time when after 1975 he became the least loved Conservative in the House of Commons, in the country at large he was rapidly being elevated into a man for all seasons.' The second part of that statement is surely correct; but the first must not be taken quite literally. These judgments about the alleged unpopularity of eminent persons at a certain moment are liable to be ephemeral. Nothing could have exceeded the odium attaching to Churchill in the House of Commons after the Abdication (1936). Throughout that period I sat from time to time in the gallery and noticed the disdainful way in which he was treated when he warned the nation about the Nazi peril.

During the General Election of 1979 I was present at a large literary lunch in Leeds. Ted Heath was one of the speakers. A high proportion of the audience were women, and the vast majority of them I should judge were Conservatives. I was sitting between two ladies of much local consequence and asked them in turn who would be more popular with this audience, Ted Heath or Margaret Thatcher? The latter had already been Leader of the Conservative Party for four years. Both were certain that of the two Heath would be far more popular. I must admit that I attended a similar lunch a few months later – Mrs Thatcher had become Prime Minister in the meanwhile – and I got precisely the opposite answer. But Heath has built up a very large volume of support in the country which nothing that happens in the House of Commons can altogether destroy.

Nevertheless, his best friends – and he has more friends than is sometimes realized – are the first to concede that his present isolated situation in the House of Commons is of his own making. It is natural, perhaps, that he should feel bitter at having his place taken by Margaret Thatcher – a woman whose cause he had done a good deal to foster. But unfortunately for him there is in contrast the example of Alec Douglas-Home. He was supplanted by Ted Heath in just the same way as Ted Heath was later supplanted by Margaret Thatcher. Yet Home served loyally and efficiently under his supplanter. Precedents in this matter vary. Asquith rejected indignantly the very idea of serving under Lloyd George. Balfour served under various Prime Ministers, but after a long interval of years. Chamberlain served briefly under Churchill. The war made that, no doubt, a special case. Every big man has his little side, but Ted Heath's little side has done him lasting damage.

Ted Heath, however, has been placed in a genuinely difficult position. He is profoundly critical, personalities apart, of some of the main policies pursued by the Thatcher government. On 17 January

1984 he fired both barrels of a powerful shotgun against that government. Two quotations from the front page of *The Times* of 18 January speak for themselves:

> Mr Edward Heath last night led a Conservative rebellion against the Government's rate-capping legislation, voting with the Opposition against a three-line whip for the first time since the Conservatives were returned to power under his successor, Mrs Margaret Thatcher, in 1979.

> Mr Edward Heath said last night that the policies pursued by the Conservative Government had deepened the recession, aggravated unemployment and damaged the fabric of the economy.

Personally I sympathize with Ted Heath over both issues. I cannot help remembering, moreover, that Churchill made himself just as big a nuisance to the Baldwin/Chamberlain governments. And everyone now says how wise and brave he was. I confine myself here to the comment that his personal attitude to Mrs Thatcher gives a most unfortunate handle to his critics. And twice in one day is rather a lot! He was soon at it again. *The Times* on 20 February 1984 carried the headline 'Heath warning on Thatcher policies'. Mr Heath, in an interview with *The Times*, had warned the Prime Minister against the dangers of pursuing a policy confrontation,

> Consensus had now become a dirty word in some quarters.

At the centenary luncheon of the parliamentary lobby recently, Mrs Thatcher had said that she wished to be known as the person who had abolished consensus. But Mr Heath said,

> We always have to remember that in a democracy a time may come when the position of those in power will change. If a bitter legacy of nonconsultation is left behind then those who take over will be animated by a similar spirit which cannot be good for the country as a whole.

Sound thinking again, in my eyes, but no one who talks that way about the views of their Party leader is likely to be regarded as a loyalist.

One must not give the impression that Heath since 1975 has been sulking in his tent in the manner of Achilles. The latter, one gathers from Homer, lay fallow. Ted Heath to start with has not only written the three books mentioned but has travelled ceaselessly and far in promoting them in signing sessions and otherwise. Although he has the reputation, not unjustified, of being shy with acquaintances, he is exceptionally forthcoming in these promotional activities. His speeches are spiced with the wit that he has never lacked since the days of the Oxford Union. He has given each of his book-purchasers in the course of these brief encounters a feeling of real friendliness and empathy.

In 1972 Andrew Roth published a book called *Heath and The Heath Men* which, though by no means above criticism, makes some points suggestively. He lays considerable stress on the fact that Ted Heath was the first Conservative Prime Minister of what he calls working-class origin. His father started as a carpenter and finished as a master-builder. His mother had been a housemaid, her father a poor and illiterate farm-worker. Ted Heath's mother, to whom he has always attributed much of his success, died when he was thirty-five and already an MP. This was a heartbreaking experience. Roth uses it (unconvincingly) to explain his allegedly 'buttoned-up' character through lack of mother love. Roth argues that

> Edward Heath's personality has been distorted by his social repression. He was born a carpenter's son in the class-conscious town of Broadstairs. His own preoccupation with the higher status of his 'betters' was unconsciously sharpened by the anxiety of his ambitious parents to 'get on', in their differing ways. This meant that he could never 'be himself', but must always pretend to a middle-class status not really his.

There may or may not be something in the point. Certainly his background was very different from that of previous Conservative Prime Ministers in this century. Salisbury and Balfour, aristocrats; Bonar Law, Baldwin and Chamberlain, prosperous businessmen; Eden, Macmillan and Home, aristocrats again. But, as we are all aware, one representative of what I would call the lower middle classes, Ted Heath, would in due course be replaced by another one, Margaret Thatcher.

By 1955 Ted Heath was Government Chief Whip. In 1959 he became Minister of Labour with a seat in Harold Macmillan's Cabinet. In 1960 he was appointed Lord Privy Seal at the Foreign Office, much concerned with the attempt to enter Europe. By 1965 Alec Home, after losing the 1964 General Election, was under considerable pressure to resign. He was supposed not to be able to stand up to Wilson effectively. I have little doubt myself that he could have survived if he had thought it dignified to fight for his position tooth and nail. The way was therefore wide-open for challengers. Heath had already established himself as a politician of all-round competence, equally at home in foreign and domestic affairs. He had played a major role in attacking the Labour budget. If Home had to go, Heath was the obvious choice, though Maudling had many talents. 'Ted's good,' said Carrington, my opposite number in the House of Lords.

At the time of writing we cannot tell whether Ted Heath will ever again occupy a high position in British politics. For the purposes of this book we must judge him today on his record as Prime Minister, 1970–4. As an ardent 'European' myself, I salute him in the first place as the man who negotiated our entry into Europe and carried the arrangements through the House of Commons in the face of a great deal of Labour hostility. He had long been the outstanding 'European' in British politics, though his Balliol near-contemporary Roy Jenkins had done almost as much for the cause.

When Churchill was removed from the key position in the Cabinet in 1915 Kitchener called on him and said, 'You had the Fleet ready; no one can take that away from you.' No one can take away from Ted Heath the largest share of the credit for bringing Britain into Europe. We had missed many chances from the time when Adenauer in 1950 begged me to persuade Attlee and Bevin to join the Schuman Plan. I got nowhere. Afterwards we were twice rebuffed by de Gaulle. Then at last the chance was there, and it was appropriate that Ted Heath was available to seize it.

Another step he took was less premeditated and more audacious. Early in 1972 his patience with the Unionist Government in Northern Ireland was exhausted. He considered rightly that they were unable or unwilling to do much justice to the Catholic minority. He suspended Stormont. By the end of the next year he was able to bring about the Sunningdale Agreement in conjunction with the Dublin Government and in consultation with the Northern Unionists under Faulkner. By that time I had myself been writing and talking about the so-called Irish problem for forty years. For the first time I permitted myself a delighted cry of unrestrained optimism. Not long before I had completed, with a colleague, a joint life of De Valera. In matters of this world De Valera was not an optimist, but after Sunningdale he told me that for the first time he saw some hope of a United Ireland coming about in his lifetime.

For a while all went well. The Joint Executive, the subordinate government set up in Northern Ireland, demonstrated – though it should never have been doubted – that given the chance Protestants and Catholics could work as well together there as anywhere else. But the most promising experiment ever undertaken in Northern Ireland was sabotaged by the Ulster Workers' Strike. For his creation of the Joint Executive, Heath, notably assisted by Whitelaw, deserves the highest praise. Its destruction can in no way be attributed to him directly. He had fallen from office by the time it occurred.

It may be said, however, that if he had not called a General

Election at that moment the Executive might have survived. Those who consider that the Election was in any case badly timed will find in its effect on Northern Ireland an additional ground of criticism. It has been suggested that in the Sunningdale Agreement the Northern Unionist leader Faulkner was pressurized into giving away too much; that the possibility of a United Ireland was allowed to loom too large. In retrospect that is probably true. But one is reluctant to blame Heath for not realizing that Faulkner could not bring his own people along with him.

So far, then, I am crediting Heath with two alpha marks, for our entry into Europe and for his handling of Northern Ireland. It is difficult to find much more to praise on the larger issues. After the loss of the two elections in 1974 Heath was bound to come under heavy criticism from within his own party, just as Home had done nine years earlier. It seems likely that there was nothing much that he could do to secure his survival. We must also bear in mind that 1970 seems, when looking back, to have been a kind of turning-point in the economic history of the Western world. The unprecedented rate of growth during the previous twenty-five years was coming to an end even before the oil crisis of 1973. That oil crisis was much the most disastrous event in the post-war era; the cost of Britain's oil imports was quadrupled. Heath in England and Nixon in America were equally stricken.

That said, and those allowances made, the economic story of Britain under Heath does not make good reading. In Opposition and again during the election campaign, Heath and his Shadow Cabinet had insisted that the general economic strategy of the Conservatives would be quite different from that of Labour. Labour's approach would be totally reversed. Lame ducks would go to the wall. Much else would be altered. But in the event, and even before the oil crisis of 1973, the plans were not working out as intended.

Iain Macleod, the Conservative Chancellor of the Exchequer upon whom many hopes were pinned, died almost at once. Anthony Barber took his place, undeniably a man of Heath's persuasion. During 1971 the economy continued in a depressed condition. The unemployment total was approaching one million – then considered intolerable, though we have learnt to live with three million since. In March 1972 Barber introduced a highly reflationary budget, but as time went on nothing seemed to go right. Inflation rose alarmingly, and bitter confrontation with the unions over the Industrial Relations Act produced a fundamental cleavage in the nation, which was in no way what Heath desired. The Heath Government were forced to make a complete about-turn over their economic policies. It seems fair to accept the summary of Sked and Cook in their *Post War Britain*:

> These economic problems forced the Goverment to abandon many of the intitiatives they had started in 1970 and to adopt policies similar to those which they had attacked so vehemently when they had been in Opposition. This was particularly the case in the fields of regional policy, consumer protection and prices and incomes policy. Likewise on the industrial front the Government was driven into a massive reversal of their original intentions. The two most spectacular instances were the saving of Rolls Royce, which had run into trouble over a fixed-price contract for the delivery of RB11 Engines for the American Lockheed Tristar, and the rescue of Upper Clyde Shipbuilders.

But all these adjustments and expedients were in vain. The oil crisis arrived in 1973 to pile on the agony. By 1974 Heath was involved in a major showdown with the miners, supported by the trade-union movement. The country lay in the grip of the three-day week. Heath – in desperation, it seems – initiated a General Election early in 1974. He was confident that the question, 'Who governs Britain?' – in other words, 'Are we going to be dictated to by the trade unions?' – would produce a Conservative victory. But he proved mistaken. The Labour Party obtained more seats than the Conservatives, though neither now nor at a later election in the same year did they have on paper a workable majority over all parties. There was, however, no combination in Parliament to overthrow them. They struggled on for five years under Wilson and Callaghan. They were evicted by Margaret Thatcher in 1979, and rebuffed still more decisively by her in 1983. In 1975 Heath had himself been ejected from the leadership.

Ted Heath after his two election defeats in 1974 was inevitably subjected to a number of different criticisms and grouses, some of them contradictory. It was easy to criticize him for his tactical handling of the dispute with the miners and his timing of the election. A much more fundamental divergence on the higher levels in his own party was brought out in the first instance by Sir Keith Joseph, who had been a prominent member of the Heath Cabinet. On 5 September 1974, with a second election still pending, Sir Keith spelt out in detail his conversion to *laissez-faire* economics and what might be called the diehard cause. Inflation, he suggested, was a self-inflicted wound. It had been primarily the result of post-war governments creating new money out of proportion to the additional goods and services available. If this made him a monetarist, then, Sir Keith said, he acquiesced in the description. Inflationary pressure had been created by successive governments because politicians were haunted by the fear of long-term mass unemployment. Sir Keith made it plain that he regarded inflation as a much greater evil.

From that time on an ideological war was publicly and privately fought between the diehards such as Keith Joseph and those who came to be called the 'wets'. The latter might reasonably appeal to the ideas of the post-war Churchill, Eden, Macmillan and Butler and the other formulators of post-war Conservatism. As we will see when we reach Mrs Thatcher, there is more than one idea involved in what came to be Thatcherism. Monetarism is the financial aspect, but the principle of restricting the role of the State and encouraging self-help was more fundamental. So was the assault on trade-union powers. No one, unless it be Mrs Thatcher herself, could illustrate better the virtue of self-help than Ted Heath himself. But, personalities apart, the gale of Conservative opinion was by this time blowing in a direction which would sweep him away. He could not, unfortunately, claim for his consensus politics that they had produced national agreement. The three-day week and the unsuccessful showdown with the miners left him with the unhappy fact of confrontation.

Which brings one finally to the psychology of this unusual man, surely the most enigmatic of all our recent Prime Ministers. Let me repeat something said earlier. He has been in my first-hand experience a great success with the general public – that is, broadly speaking, an audience of strangers. I also know quite well at least half a dozen (and I am sure that there are many more) established friends of his who will never lose their admiration and affection for him, however trying they find some of his attitudes. But one of these has told me that, after working with Ted Heath for a long time in the closest fashion, he knows him no better than when they came together. The mass of MPs without even that amount of access to his mind are bound to put his extreme reserve down to coldness.

Some years ago I read in the morning papers that he had been recently successful in getting his weight down. I met him in a restaurant and addressed him cheerfully, 'Hello, Ted, how's the weight?' thinking that it would be a welcome inquiry. He replied coolly, 'All right. How's yours?' I had known him so long that I did not feel snubbed; a young unseasoned Member of Parliament might have reacted differently.

At the time of his fall he was sometime accused of unduly dominating his Cabinet. But the same might have been said of Chamberlain, the wartime Churchill, Macmillan and today of Margaret Thatcher. He has been described as displaying a military style of leadership and perhaps that is a reasonable description. He is far too intelligent a man, however, to think that he could run the whole country himself. From various talks he has given since, including a radio dialogue with Lord Trend, a former Secretary of the Cabinet, it is clear that he has given much thought to how a Prime Minister should get the best out of his team. He himself has proved most successful in that respect in the worlds of sailing and music.

I compare him in my own mind with Richard Nixon, not only because each of them has received much less than his deserts. Having myself written a book on Nixon and taken the chair for him on two occasions when he was addressing well-informed audiences on world affairs, I would submit that there is no one in our time who exhibits at his best so wide and deep a grasp of international politics. I am ready to place Ted Heath in the same class, though his opportunities have been much narrower.

Since Heath ceased to be leader of the Conservative Party he has lectured at home and abroad on international questions with rare knowledge and perspicacity. The famous Brandt Report on the relations between northern and southern hemispheres owes an enormous amount to him. He finished as the joint chairman. I would not be surprised to hear that he had written most of the report himself.

His thinking is on that kind of level. It is a sad reflection that 'a little local difficulty' in chatting up rank-and-file MPs should be depriving the world of the services of one who is so outstandingly equipped to benefit humanity.

James Callaghan

The Avuncular Man

CALLAGHAN
Rt Hon. (Leonard) James
(1912–   )

M.P. (Lab.) South Cardiff, 1945–50, South-East Cardiff since 1950

Parliamentary Secretary, Ministry of Transport, 1947–50;
Chairman, Committee on Road Safety, 1948–50;
Parliamentary and Financial Secretary, Admiralty, 1950–1;
Chancellor of the Exchequer, 1964–7;
Home Secretary, 1967–70;
Secretary of State for Foreign and Commonwealth Affairs, 1974–6;
Minister of Overseas Development, 1975–6;
Prime Minister and First Lord of the Treasury, 1976–9.
Leader of the Opposition, 1979–80.

The Avuncular Man

THE SCENE IS THE Labour Party Conference 1983. The debate on international affairs is drawing to an end, with just about the usual amount of pleasant excitement. Suddenly a familiar figure, strongly made but now somewhat bowed, is seen to be making its way to the platform amid a mounting chorus of boos. It is Jim Callaghan, who has spoken so well and acceptably at so many conferences. This time it is different.

In the General Election he had erupted suddenly, in the course of his own candidature, with a firm statement of opposition to unilateral disarmament, a restatement in fact of the line he had taken as Prime Minister, and for many years before that. A great howl had gone up from the Labour activists, as no doubt he expected. He unmercifully uncovered the cracks in the foreign and defence policy of the party, which the leaders at that time were desperately anxious to paper over. But knowing Jim Callaghan for so long, and having spoken to him recently on these matters, I would have been surprised if he had not come out in just that way.

At the Party Conference he was for a long time silent, 'the dog that didn't bark in the night'. Some agreement had apparently been reached between Jim and the platform that he would refrain from speaking, if he was not personally attacked. The arrangement nearly worked out, but almost at the end of the foreign policy and defence debate a speaker made remarks about him which he rightly regarded as offensive. He insisted on replying.

The antagonism of the hall, so different from his previous receptions, cannot have been pleasant. He remained urbane as always. He restated his position and underlined it, without unnecessary provocation. Immediately afterwards, I went up to him outside the hall. I joined the little group patting him on the back. He looked happy and relaxed, much more so I am sure than if he had had to keep his thoughts to himself.

All our other post-war Prime Ministers were educated at Oxford. They obtained first-class, second-class or third-class degrees. Whatever their academic achievements their minds had all been trained in a certain fashion. Callaghan's education was quite different and ended much earlier. He was born in 1912 and brought up in the West Country. His father was a chief petty officer in the Navy whose family originally came from Ireland. His mother imbued him early with strong Noncomformist principles. He was educated at elementary and secondary schools. By seventeen he was a tax inspector in the Civil Service, by twenty-four he was Assistant Secretary of the Inland Revenue's Staff Federation. By donnish standards (there were half a dozen men with Oxford first classes in Wilson's Cabinet) he was a badly educated man. Dick Crossman used to talk privately of Callaghan as a man not fully capable of understanding economics, when he was Chancellor of the Exchequer. But Dick himself had had no economic training. He was utterly brilliant in most respects, but so bad at mathematics that although he won a scholarship to Oxford, he had to find an alternative way of entry which did not include mathematics. In my experience, Callaghan, with his training in the Inland Revenue, understood practical economics better than nine Chancellors out of ten, and was probably more at home in tax matters than any of them.

Dick Crossman, for all his constant sniping at Callaghan in his diaries, recognizes almost with awe that in political skill Callaghan was his superior, and this no doubt was true. Partly perhaps because he had not been to Oxford and had been educated therefore to the same sort of level as the great majority of the population, he had a deep instinctive understanding of popular feeling, greater perhaps than that of any of our other ten Prime Ministers. Churchill and Neville Chamberlain had not, it is true, been to university, but both of them had been brought up in circles very close to the top of the greasy pole. Of the nine individuals who have become Prime Minister since the war, seven were educated at Oxford. Only Churchill and Callaghan were denied that privilege. When I resigned from the Cabinet in 1968 because of the postponement of the raising of the school-leaving age, he spoke movingly on my side as one who had had to leave school far too early. So, I may add, did George Brown.

One must not forget to mention here Callaghan's wartime service in the Navy. I would not be able to measure its effect on him, but it has obviously been profound. It has in the first place given him a point of contact with the population as a whole, including his Conservative adversaries, which has been denied to a man like Wilson, whose war service in Whitehall was probably of more value to the nation but of less value to him. There is discernible also in Callaghan the special form of patriotism which could never tolerate, even in thought, a policy that threatened (however slightly) the defences of the country.

He was Parliamentary Secretary (Under-Secretary) at the Admiralty when I became First Lord in 1951. There were not a few, including Jim himself, who felt that it was he who deserved the top position. But he was always completely loyal to me. I have since been told that the admirals formed the opinion that he would one day be Prime Minister. However, he had been on the scene a long time before that came about in 1976.

He had been a member of the House of Commons for over thirty years (since 1945). No other Prime Minister in this century, except Winston Churchill, had to wait so long (Churchill had to wait forty years, with a two-year break from 1922 to 1924). In the nineteenth century, Disraeli had had to wait for about the same time as Callaghan.

He had the unique distinction of having held the three most glamorous posts after the premiership. He had been Chancellor of the Exchequer (1964–7), Home Secretary (1967–70) and Foreign Secretary (1974–6). In all these high positions he had looked the part and held his own comfortably enough with contemporary leaders at home and abroad.

He was a big, burly man, friendly and avuncular in aspect. In later years a slight stoop, a slow, measured tread and large horn-rimmed glasses completed the picture of a popular leader. His family life was a model. He was at all times the thoroughly decent man. He had an easy word for everyone, but never gave the impression of unduly courting popularity.

When one says that someone is a consummate politician there is apt to be a slight suggestion of the man in the story who said at the end of his speech: 'Those are my principles. If you don't like them, I can always change them.' No doubt there is a flexibility in Callaghan which is comparable to that of Harold Wilson, but in Callaghan it causes less offence, because it seems to be based less on calculation than on instinct. He is certainly not a man who for most of the time is trying to impose his ideas on those he is working with. But he is an obstinate man, and where his convictions are involved he does not budge easily. When he became Prime Minister he deliberately set out to adhere more strictly to principle than either Macmillan or Wilson.

The old verse of the poet T. H. Crosland comes back to mind:

> I trod the road to Hell,
> But there were things I might have sold
> And did not sell.

There is no reason to suppose that Jim Callaghan has ever trod the road to any kind of Hell. But the famous phrase associated with Jimmy Saville, 'Jim'll fix it', has been on occasion applied to Jim Callaghan also. So it seems right to indicate that in certain wide areas he is as much as anyone, even Mrs Thatcher, a 'conviction' politician.

Jim Callaghan and Margaret Thatcher are shrewd and calculating yet thoroughly honest. If I am told that there is here a contradiction in terms I deny it vigorously. I will have on my side all those who understand the world of politics and are proud to belong to it or serve it.

Jim Callaghan is the most natural orator of all our eleven Prime Ministers. He does not possess the literary gifts of Churchill or, for that matter, Baldwin. His finest speeches do not compare with theirs. In my experience he has not had the power to sweep an audience off its feet in the manner of Aneurin Bevan, but his general level has been astonishingly high. Having heard him speak often at Labour conferences to thousands of listeners, and still more often to twenty people in Cabinet, I have recognized in him an extraordinary God-given power of finding the appropriate words without effort. Fine intellectuals like Dick Crossman and Tony Crosland made little gem-like interventions in the Cabinet, but you could almost hear their brains working. Jim Callaghan did it all so effortlessly, and, whether before a small audience or a large, carried at all times much conviction.

In *Post-war Britain*, by Alan Sked and Chris Cook, we are told that when Callaghan became Prime Minister on 5 April 1975

> few contrasts could have been more marked than that between the new premier and his predecessor. Callaghan, a chapel goer, teetotaller and non-smoker, was 64; in contrast to Wilson's brilliant academic career at Oxford, he had had only an elementary and secondary school education. . . .

The last point we have made already, but the summarization of Callaghan as chapel-goer, teetotaller and non-smoker makes one pause. Wilson is certainly associated with an ever-present pipe and enjoys a drink about as much as I do, which is quite a lot. My impression is that Jim Callaghan gave up drinking not for non-comformist reasons, but on health grounds. I applaud his strength of character that has enabled him to keep his vow where all about him are imbibing freely. The reference to him as a chapel-goer is no doubt just. But it prompts me to recall an experience in 1966, when he was Chancellor of the Exchequer and we were undergoing one of our periodic financial crises. The issue was whether we should or should not devalue the pound.

I was much exercised about the way I should vote in the Cabinet. In theory we did not have votes, but voices were collected meticulously, which came to the same thing. I was at that time Leader of the House of Lords, and a member of the main economic committee, but I had no economic advice available to me in my own office. It was easier in theory than in practice to draw on the Cabinet secretariat.

It should be recalled that when the Wilson Cabinet was first formed Wilson, in conjunction with George Brown, First Secretary of State and Secretary of State for Economic Affairs, and Callaghan, Chancellor of the Exchequer, had decided before the Cabinet ever met that we must adhere to the existing parity of sterling. The prestige of Britain and that of the Labour Party figured largely in that decision. For a long time it was *verboten* to mention devaluation in the Cabinet. Tony Crosland, when he came into the Cabinet and sat next to me, was passionately convinced that we ought to devalue, but the most that he ever said about it for a long time was to refer to it as 'the unmentionable'.

By mid-1966, however, the intellectuals in the Cabinet, as Tony Crosland would refer to them, were inclined to favour devaluation: Crosland himself, of course, but by now also Dick Crossman, George Brown, Roy Jenkins and others. Douglas Jay, however, President of the Board of Trade, as clever as any of them, and in possession of far more up-to-date statistics, stood with Wilson and Callaghan, and ultimately convinced me to support them in the Cabinet discussions, in which (perhaps unfortunately) they prevailed.

Here I am concerned with Jim Callaghan the man. I called on him at a time when his burden – already heavy – was increased by the absence of Harold Wilson the Prime Minister in Moscow. I shall not forget the absolute fairness and kindness with which he treated me. He had said more than once before then that I had always supported him in the Cabinet, which was broadly speaking true. He would have liked to have had my support this time, but he was determined that I should have every opportunity of arriving at a contrary view.

He arranged for me to see one of his special advisers, Professor Nield, to help me make up my mind. I discovered afterwards that Nield was really against the policy of Wilson – i.e., he was in favour of devaluation, but he was so loyal to his chief, Callaghan, that I was left under the impression that the arguments for devaluation should be rejected. I have never to this day known what Jim Callaghan thought about the economic issues involved. But what sticks in my mind is his intense loyalty to Wilson, though I don't suppose that the two have ever been intimate friends. 'We can't let down the PM,' or words to that effect, was what he said to me.

Later, with preternatural fairness, he sent me off to see Sir Donald McDougall, economic adviser to George Brown, and at that moment the most deadly opponent of the Wilson-Callaghan policy.

But my abiding recollection of him that morning is different. He was labouring under great strain; he trusted me, and at one point he said to me, 'You know, Frank, that I was brought up to say my prayers night and morning by my mother, a very strict Christian. I am afraid that I have fallen away in recent years. But now, for the first time for a long while, I am beginning to say them again.' I have no doubt that he has continued the practice.

On one occasion, Tony Crosland, sitting next to me in the Cabinet, took up a point with me. It arose from a speech I was to deliver that afternoon on education, he being Minister of Education at the time. 'Can you really justify your statement', he asked me, 'that we are a Christian Cabinet?' I did a quick count round the room, though much of it was inevitably guesswork. 'I make it eleven Christians, beginning with the top three – Harold Wilson, George Brown and Jim Callaghan – six non- or anti-Christians and four don't knows.'

Jim Callaghan's Christianity, like that of some of the greatest saints (St Augustine, for example) owes an immeasurable debt to his mother.

A few words about his performances as Chancellor and Home Secretary. One day the whole story of the decision to cling to the existing parity of sterling until we were literally forced off it in 1967 will be laid before us. We shall be made aware how far the responsibility was that of Wilson and how far that of Callaghan. And of course it is not presumed in this series of biographical essays to talk dogmatically, as though the original decision in 1964 to maintain the parity and the decision to stick to it in 1966 were mistaken. I myself am inclined to think that they were, but no one can say pontifically that Jim Callaghan was wrong in 1964 and again in 1966. What cannot be contested is that he behaved like a man of honour when we were forced off the parity in 1967. He insisted on resigning to keep faith with those all over the world who had relied on his word that we would not devalue. He allowed himself (rightly, I would say) to be dissuaded from leaving the Cabinet altogether. He accepted the slight demotion of becoming Home Secretary. On leaving No. 11 Downing Street, his political career was damaged seriously, but he could hold his head as high as ever.

He will be remembered at the Home Office most of all perhaps for his positive attitude to the problems of Northern Ireland. That province was still without a Minister of its own. He has given us a vivid picture in his book about Northern Ireland of the low priority it then occupied in his new department. In spite of his name (his father's family came from southern Ireland), he had been brought up in an atmosphere of West Country noncomformity. He told the House of Commons on one occasion that he grew up without much respect for Catholics. But the injustices suffered by the Catholics in the north came home readily to a man of his human sensibility.

He took over the Home Office when the long discrimination against the Catholic minority was at last producing a horrifying confrontation. It was he who, with the approval of Harold Wilson, took the decisive step in August 1969 of sending in the British Army to protect the Catholics. They were in danger of grave maltreatment, possibly even massacre, by the Protestant majority. Callaghan himself went over soon afterwards and won golden opinions, particularly among the Catholics. No one can say what would have happened if the Conservatives had not won the Westminster elections in 1970. Thereafter, the situation deteriorated rapidly.

Ulster Unionist ministers told me at the time, when I visited the province in July 1970, that they felt that they now had a free hand to treat the minority in the correct manner, whatever that might mean. The strength of the IRA, negligible in August 1969, rapidly escalated. It may be felt that Callaghan moved too slowly to promote reforms, but his departure was bitterly regretted by the Catholic minority, who felt that a real source of protection had been taken away.

Apart from his Northern Ireland policies, one would not remember anything very distinctive about Jim Callaghan's performance at the Home Office. Roy Jenkins, his predecessor, emerges with a slightly exaggerated reputation as a penal reformer. He undoubtedly had his heart in what penal reformers would call the right place. He carried through various reforms which had already been set in motion by his predecessor, Frank Soskice. They largely derived in principle from the proposals of a Labour Party committee, of which I was chairman, before the Wilson Government was formed. They included, for example, the historic introduction of the parole system. We had of course recommended the abolition of capital punishment, which was carried out in effect in the time of the Wilson Government before Callaghan became Home Secretary. That would no doubt have happened in any case, whether our committee had or had not existed.

When Jim Callaghan became Home Secretary he invited me as an already established penal reformer to come and make suggestions to him. Looking back, I missed my chance. I have always found it difficult to set aside the long-term view and propose the kind of immediate changes which are all that one can expect from the average Home Secretary.

The one bold stand with which I associate Callaghan as Home Secretary is his blunt rejection of the Wootton Report which would have reduced penalties for possessing cannabis. The action and still more the words with which he accompanied it in 1969 were very significant in view of the rapid movement towards the permissive society in the 1960s, strongly encouraged by Home Secretary Roy Jenkins.

He was glad, said Jim Callaghan, that his decision against the report, which seemed to be generally approved, had enabled the House to call a halt to the advancing tide of social permissiveness. 'I regard it', he said, 'as one of the most unlikeable words that has been invented in recent years. If only we would regard ourselves as a compassionate society, an unselfish society, I would feel prouder of 1969.' I myself wrote in a book published in 1974 that the phrase 'permissive society' seemed from about that time to become discredited. I went on, however, to say that it would be premature to assume that the intellectual pressures it represented had spent themselves.

I myself initiated a debate in the Lords in 1971 and, following that, a prolonged Inquiry into pornography. We reported in 1972. I would not care to dogmatize as to whether the evil side of the permissive society (and it has had a virtuous side as well) had been more or less pronounced since Jim Callaghan spoke in 1969. But at least he did all he could at that moment to stem the tide.

The one serious blot on his record in the last years of the Wilson Cabinet was not departmental. As indicated above, Barbara Castle, Secretary of State for Employment and Productivity, made a bold and enlightened effort to deal with unofficial strikes. Callaghan was the most prominent of the Ministers who secured the defeat of that policy. He was to pay a heavy price later on, when he himself was Prime Minister.

We move on to 1976. He took over from Harold Wilson under circumstances which could hardly have been more discouraging. At the second election in 1974, Labour had finished up with 319 seats in a House of 635. The situation on paper became still worse as the by-elections went against Labour. On paper, there was after a time no majority of any kind. It was possible however (and this Callaghan achieved) to keep afloat by an agreement with the Liberals. The Liberals gained more influence at Westminster than for many years, though in the country their fortunes underwent a disastrous slump.

Callaghan also (and for this I blame him, whereas I praise him for his alliance with the Liberals) did a 'deal' with the Ulster Unionists, under which Northern Ireland as a whole secured another five seats at Westminster. Knowing as I do what the Labour Party have always felt, and continue to feel about the Ulster Unionists, I regard this particular bargain as below his standard – an attempt to stay in power at all costs. No doubt it seemed a duty.

Whether or not Labour had had a strong position in the House of Commons, Callaghan was presented with a painful economic legacy. Labour had laid much stress during the elections of 1974 on their power to reach and carry out a social contract with the unions. But by the time Callaghan took over the situation of the economy was desperate. In July 1976, to avert a further fall in the value of sterling, substantial cuts were announced in the Government's spending plans for 1977–8 and interest rates were raised to record levels. These measures were not sufficient, however, to prevent a dramatic slide in the pound during the autumn, which forced the government to seek a $3,900 million loan from the International Monetary Fund. To obtain this assistance increases in taxation and further cuts in public expenditure, amounting to £3,000 million over the next two years, were imposed in December.

The sterling crisis of 1976 marked the low point of the Government's struggle with the economy. During 1977 and 1978 the benefits of North Sea oil began to transform the balance of payments. To quote Sked and Chris Cook in *Post-war Britain*:

> For 1977 as a whole the balance of payments showed a surplus of £1 million. The pound was riding high – helped partly by the continuing weakness of the dollar. Even the rate of inflation – though uncomfortably high in comparison with Britain's major competitors – was at least reduced to single figures. The signs of economic recovery were reflected in the April 1978 budget, with its modest reductions in personal taxation and its mildly expansionary aims.

Unemployment was very heavy, though less than half of what it is at the time of writing in 1983. But measures of social value had been carried through in spite of the pitifully small majority. The Police Act, a Health Services Act, an Education Act, a Race Relations Act, to mention only a few. If Callaghan had gone to the country in the autumn of 1978, as was generally expected, it would have been hard to fault his record.

As it was, he carried on through what came to be known as 'the winter of discontent', of which the refuse lying uncollected in the streets was the visible embodiment. The attempt of his Government to restrict the increase of the wages of public employees and the resulting chaos illustrated once again the failure of all governments to find a way of keeping wage demands to a reasonable level in an age of full employment. It was not surprising perhaps that a Conservative Government should at this point be returned to power with a recipe that was totally different.

Callaghan may or not have chosen the right moment for an election. Those who lose elections – Attlee in 1951, Heath in 1974, Callaghan in 1979 – are always accused of disastrous timing. But he had done enough to win an honourable place, if not one of surpassing distinction, in the long line of Prime Ministers. The cards were heavily stacked against him.

Margaret Thatcher

The Family Governess

THATCHER
Rt Hon. (Hilda) Margaret
(1925–   )

M.P. (C) Barnet, Finchley, since 1974 (Finchley, 1959–74).

Joint Parliamentary Secretary, Ministry of Pensions and
National Insurance, 1961–4;
Secretary of State for Education and Science, 1970–4;
Leader of the Opposition, 1975–9;
Prime Minister and First Lord of the Treasury, since 1979.

The Family Governess

MARGARET THATCHER GOES DOWN IN history indisputably as the first woman in Britain to be Prime Minister. No one enjoying a *tête-à-tête* with her, official or otherwise, can fail to be aware of her sex, or suppose that she is unaware of it herself. Other Prime Ministers, Eden and Macmillan for example, have taken a good deal of trouble over their appearance, but no one compares with her in her evident desire to make the most of her physical appeal, in her case her feminine charm. It may well be that for many years she was conscious of the disadvantage of being a woman in politics. Whether it was so or not, she has put that right long ago.

Her hair is done freshly each day. She makes a more pleasing impression than even the most handsome of our male Prime Ministers. One should add that she has fully discharged at all times the duties of a devoted wife and mother. It appears that her husband Denis, the most friendly of men, does indeed call her 'the boss' as he is depicted as doing in *Private Eye*. That would not suit every husband, but it would be hard to improve on the Thatchers as a family unit.

She has experienced a good measure of triumph and near-disaster but she has always responded to adversity with courage and resilience.

Margaret Roberts, as she then was, was born in October 1925. She is a few months older than the Queen. She is the daughter of the late Alfred Roberts, the famous grocer of Grantham who became mayor of the town. She was educated at the Kesteven and Grantham Girls' school and won her way thence to Somerville College, Oxford.

She was not an outstanding student at Oxford. Maybe she chose the wrong subject in chemistry. She felt the strain of 'schools' so intensely that she had to write the first examination paper in a bed in the sanatorium. She rapidly recovered and wrote the other papers in the examination schools. She obtained a basic second-class degree.

She was soon adopted as a Conservative candidate for Dartford – not, it would seem, a winnable seat. She fought it in 1950 and a second time in 1951, on each occasion unsuccessfully. It was not until the summer of 1959 that she struck lucky and obtained a seat

(Finchley) which she duly won in the election of that year. In the meanwhile she had been turned down by a number of constituencies. Most of us would have given up the idea of a political career, but not Margaret Roberts by any means.

She was Parliamentary Secretary at the Ministry of Pensions and National Insurance 1961–4, and from 1970–74 Secretary of State for Education and Science. When Minister of Education, Margaret Thatcher aroused the ire of a large section of the population by stopping free milk in primary schools. The *Sun*, later to laud her to the skies, called her the most unpopular woman in Britain. She was labelled 'Mrs Thatcher, milk-snatcher'. She was physically assaulted; a stone egg produced an enormous bruise on her chest. 'Did it hurt?' she was asked. 'It did hurt like mad,' she admitted. 'And what did you do?' 'I went on speaking,' said Margaret, 'what else could I do?' She confessed later that she was almost broken by the experience. Denis, most staunch of husbands, was saying that perhaps the time had come for Margaret to give it all up (this was in 1971), but I cannot believe that she ever entertained the idea of such a surrender. Within the higher reaches of the Tory Party, she was as unpopular as anywhere else, but ironically enough, in view of future events, it was Ted Heath who saved her. He had consistently pushed her forward. Now he dug in his heels and insisted that she should stay in office, when he could easily have thrown her to the wolves. Tory wives thoroughly disliked her at that time.

I have said before now, in the House of Lords for example, that no Prime Minister in this century has dominated a Cabinet in peacetime as she has done. But studying, for the purposes of this book, her predecessors, I hesitate to repeat that judgment in such an unqualified form. I leave out the wartime Churchill by definition; the peacetime Churchill was barely in control. But Neville Chamberlain dominated his Cabinet, and so did Macmillan. Chamberlain decided on a new foreign policy, just as Margaret Thatcher decided on a new economic and social policy.

Chamberlain's foreign policy broke down, while hers, in the eyes of her supporters and the 1983 electors, can be said to have succeeded. (Not that I see it in that way myself.) She has eliminated the 'wets' from her Cabinet quite ruthlessly. Chamberlain treated Eden in a fashion that made his resignation inevitable. It is true that he operated in conjunction with three special allies in the Cabinet – Halifax, Hoare and Simon – but he was at all times the master up to the moment of catastrophe. The similarity between his approach to his colleagues and hers is fairly marked. But she is far more of a populist than he ever was, or could have been. She has been much more successful than he was in arousing public sympathy.

Not that she has been consistently popular since she was Prime Minister. There was a point in 1981 when, according to the opinion polls, she was more unpopular than any Prime Minister in recorded history. Before the Falklands War there was a moment when one of the shrewdest political judges, William Rees-Mogg, was ready to wager a magnum of champagne that the Alliance would obtain more seats in the next General Election than any other party. The Falklands War changed all that. We slipped into it through the incompetence of her Government, but she provided forceful leadership and, for the time at least, won the enthusiasm of the nation. The opinion polls tell an interesting story.

In April 1982 35 per cent of the public were satisfied with her as Prime Minister. In July 52 per cent. I can think of no like transformation .

The General Election of 1983 was an indubitable triumph for her. Since then her Government, up to the time of writing, has enjoyed varied fortunes. But taking the whole five years, she is entitled to claim (though the claim will be vehemently resisted) that her method of running the Cabinet has proved remarkably effective. Macmillan was, like Chamberlain, a very masterful Prime Minister, but the adjective masterful does not seem to have a feminine equivalent.

Like Chamberlain and Margaret Thatcher, Macmillan dealt roughly with those whose policies did not fit in with his own ideas. He accepted cheerfully the resignations of his three Treasury ministers when they seemed too anxious to achieve financial economies. He dismissed Selwyn Lloyd, his Chancellor of the Exchequer, again because he also seemed to be following Treasury principles rather than Macmillan's persistent preference for expansionism. For good measure, Macmillan got rid of another six Cabinet ministers at the same time. Margaret Thatcher has never achieved quite so much at a stroke, but for one reason or another we have seen the departure of Carrington, Soames, Pym, Gilmour, Norman St John Stevas and others. It is generally accepted that in her Cabinet you toe the line or you are out.

There has been nothing in my experience to compare with the drastic break that she has made between her policies and those of past Conservative leaders. Not even lip service has been paid by her and her immediate entourage, ('the poisonous ideologues' of Norman St John Stevas's phrase) to the glorious Conservative traditions. All Conservatives are capable of using Disraeli for their own purposes, but there does not seem to have been much attempt to demonstrate that Thatcherism is derived from him.

Her father, the grocer of Grantham who in due course became mayor, had tremendous influence on her. He was a devout Methodist. Margaret, as a girl, was given the strictest of religious upbringings. Sunday was entirely given over to the church. Margaret and her sister Muriel attended Finkin Street Methodist Church, a ten-minute walk away, four times most Sundays: Sunday School at 10.00, followed an hour later by morning service, where they joined their parents; home for lunch, then back again for another session of Sunday School at 2.30 p.m., at which Margaret sometimes played the piano; finally an evening service at 6.00.

In due course her father moved from Liberalism to Conservatism, but John Nott, Minister of Defence during the Falklands period, has described himself as an old-fashioned Liberal and said that Margaret Thatcher is at heart the same. A little while ago Margaret Thatcher, who has not, as far as I know, studied the history of economic or political thought, suddenly emerged with a prolonged eulogy of Adam Smith, whose classical book *The Wealth of Nations* (1776) has inspired the economists of the free market ever since. But one is aware that many streams of thought have contributed to modern Conservatism. Harold Macmillan in his essay on the Whig position tells with gusto the story of Lord Lansdowne, who had held many of the highest offices in the State as a Conservative leader, declining to enter the Carlton Club, although the alternative was to be drenched in a downpour of rain. By no possible use of words can Mrs Thatcher point to herself as the inheritor of Conservative traditions and, to be fair to her, she has never made the attempt.

Margaret Thatcher must be described (in a complimentary rather than a pejorative sense) as a moralist politician, the first on the highest level since Gladstone. I take for granted her private life, which is exemplary, like that of all our leaders as far as we can tell since Lloyd George, who cannot receive that accolade. I am suggesting, however, that Mrs Thatcher is a *preacher* of morals. She is deliberately setting out to improve the moral standards of this country by exhortation and, where possible, by government action. It goes without saying that no more than in the case of Gladstone are her political opponents prepared to accept her sermons as inspired text.

She has for some years, and long before the Falklands crisis, called for a return to the ancient virtues of self-help, self-discipline and self-sacrifice. No one questions her own powers of self-help and self-discipline, and anyone who renounces, as she has done, a quarter of her salary must be listened to with respect on the subject of self-sacrifice. She leaves a clear impression that she considers that the principle of self-sacrifice has been undervalued for many years. But when her moral convictions lead her into the field of social morality they become extremely controversial.

Here, however, we must pause and try to go a little deeper. Penny Junor in her excellent biography ends her final chapter with a strong assertion of the nature of Margaret Thatcher's leadership.

> The hallmark of Margaret Thatcher's leadership is her strong and fundamental belief in the Christian ethic. Some say that she has been the first fully committed Christian Prime Minister since Lord Salisbury, who died in 1903. She has certainly taken a far greater hand in episcopal matters than any First Lord of the Treasury has been wont in recent times; and her policies can all be seen to follow the very basic tenets of right and wrong that were learned without question in the Methodist church in Finkin Street. The importance she attaches to her marriage and to the family is also part of the same pattern, as is her belief that people should be allowed to develop according to their own talents, and be permitted the freedom of choice that the Christian faith holds so dear.

There is more than one point to be taken up here. It is downright wrong to say that 'she has been the first fully committed Christian Prime Minister since Lord Salisbury, who died in 1903'. Of the eleven under our consideration, one could not call Neville Chamberlain a Christian. He was officially a Unitarian, but a Unitarian historian declined to treat him as such on the grounds that there was no evidence that he was attached to a Unitarian church. Churchill's religion could be argued about interminably without a satisfactory conclusion. I have no idea where Eden comes in this discussion.

Attlee, as we have seen, said of himself, 'I accept the Christian ethic; but can't accept the mumbo jumbo.' But there is no sense in which, on the face of it, the other six Prime Ministers could be said to be less Christian than Margaret Thatcher. According to Penny Junor, her attendance at church at Chequers was better than that of her predecessors. (The Homes were not there often.)

I have quoted above Alec Home's Christian witness. I should be surprised if Mrs Thatcher would ever have articulated her faith in this way. The truth is that she is a sincere but unintellectual Christian. She has retained and tried to apply in the highest places her childhood religion. But there is nothing in anything of hers that I have read, or any public evidence, that she has thought about Christianity in the way that she has thought about the great political issues.

She once said, 'Our religion teaches us that every human being is unique and must play his part in working out his own salvation. So, whereas socialists begin with society, and how people can be fitted in, we must start with man, whose social and economic relationships are just part of his wider existence.'

All that is very crude. It is the kind of thing one says on a political platform. When I was a Conservative I tried to believe that it was true. Now, for many years, I have argued in elections that socialism is the practical expression of Christianity. Socialism in an ideal form would be nothing less. The same message has been proclaimed on the Labour side by men like George Lansbury, Stafford Cripps, and my great friend Donald Soper. Conservative Christians, even more devout, as far as one can judge, than Mrs Thatcher, like Lord Halifax and brilliant academic thinkers like Lord Hailsham, have argued precisely the opposite. Anyone who has attended prayers in either House of Parliament is aware that equally sincere Christians can rise from their knees and in a few moments be vigorously opposing one another in debating controversy. It is part of Mrs Thatcher's strength, but surely a large part also of her weakness, that she can dismiss the convictions of so large a proportion of the country in such contemptuous terms. But of course that is the way of political parties, above all of party controversialists. She has already proved herself a great party politician, whose simple Christianity, the Christianity of her childhood, is as sincere as ever it was and is 'just the stuff to give the troops'.

So much for Christian policies. What of her personal motivation in politics? My mind often returns to the famous saying of Chancellor von Bülow: 'Real politicians are animated by two motives only: love of country and love of power.' Of course, that is an over-simplification. Most of us, politicians or otherwise, are governed by more motives than two. Mrs Thatcher's love of her family is unquestionable and her dedication to the 'work ethic' acquired all those years ago in Grantham has a purity of its own.

Looking calmly at our last four Prime Ministers – Wilson, Heath, Callaghan and Margaret Thatcher – we cannot overlook the fact that they made their way to the top by exceptional and prolonged exertions, starting a long way down. The previous seven were born with golden, or at least silver, spoons in their mouths, compared with the four just mentioned. It is not discreditable to say of Sebastian Coe, Steve Ovett or Steve Cram that they have dedicated themselves for many years to winning an Olympic title. No doubt they are proud to win it 'for Britain', but that can hardly be seen as the original motive. In the case of Margaret Thatcher I would not venture to strike the balance between her personal ambition and her patriotism. I am ready to agree that in the last resort she would be prepared for unlimited sacrifice in the interests of the country. I would say the same of all our selected eleven. With politicians, the matter is seldom simple. It is tempting to persuade onself 'I can save the country and nobody else can.'

Penny Junor says of Margaret Thatcher:

> In her early political career she was not driven by a desire to be Prime Minister. She had looked for someone else to save the country that she held so dear. Finding no one amongst the leaders of the Conservative Party, with the courage to lay their popularity on the line in order to take the unpalatable steps necessary to turn back the tide, she did it herself.

That is no doubt how she herself sees the story today. I can well believe that the prospect of a woman becoming Prime Minister seemed remote, but when the time came she struck out for her own hand and did not hesitate to strike down the man, Ted Heath, who had done so much to protect her interests.

What does she stand for in political terms? Four objectives as I see it, though I do not suppose that she considers them analytically. 1) Inflexible opposition to the threat of Soviet aggression. 2) Unremitting endeavour to control and eventually eliminate inflation. 3) Steely determination to reduce the power of the trade unions. 4) Fundamental dedication to private enterprise and the conditions required to make it successful. Under the last heading she assumes with a majority of the business community that public expenditure must be substantially reduced in order to relieve business of the burden of taxation. It is taken for granted that businessmen will work harder, show more enterprise and stay in the country more faithfully if their tax burden is lightened. It is assumed with rather more compelling logic that they will invest more if they are left with more free money to invest.

There is another assumption, seldom made so explicit; it is assumed that a high degree of inequality is required to make capitalism work, and that the trend of recent years towards a greater equality must be reversed.

This is not an issue on which Conservatives are particularly candid. Some years ago at a debate at the Oxford Union I argued that the Conservative Party stood for more inequality, the Labour Party for more equality. One of the Conservative ministers opposing me rose excitably and denounced me for gross distortion, the other sat quietly in his place with a shrewd look on his face. He knew that what I had said was far too true to be contradicted. His name was Michael Heseltine. Three years ago I opened the debate in the House of Lords in which I called for a much greater measure of equality. The Government's Baroness Young submerged the issue with her habitual charm. In this matter I understand the difference between the two parties only too well – if only as a renegade Conservative. Until Mrs Thatcher took over Conservative leaders favoured a consensus, but she for good or ill is an exponent of 'real' Conservatism.

As regards the Soviet menace, I share what I imagine would be her view – that it is an all too potent reality. She has struck up a warm political and, it would seem, a personal friendship with President Reagan. He has described her as 'the best man the British have got'. I hope that her attitude, misguided in my eyes, over the Grenada issue has not damaged the relationship.

Jim Callaghan, returning from a visit to Russia in 1983, suggested that the tone of her pronouncements, like those of President Reagan, was more aggressive than was required by the interests of Western defence.

There is no denying that Mrs Thatcher's pronouncements will always be emphatic and not infrequently provocative to those who disagree with them strongly. As will be suggested below, her weakness is that she tends to oversimplify highly complex issues. But in my eyes the Soviet menace is likely to remain a simple fact of life for years to come. There is much to be said for a simple reply which every citizen can understand.

On the domestic front the struggle against inflation is obviously her top priority. Mr Harold Macmillan said in a broadcast in October 1983 that a small degree of inflation is desirable rather than otherwise. It will be argued against him that the small degree of inflation during his premiership played no mean part in producing the heavy inflation with which Mrs Thatcher was left to cope. Be that as it may, her considerable success in combating inflation was a substantial achievement during her first administration. Her party were entitled to capitalize on it during the election.

Against that there has been the horrifying level of unemployment. She may be defended on the grounds that this would have been inevitable anyway in the light of the world situation. Few people seriously believe that. The reduction in inflation has been achieved at a heavy price in human distress, especially among the young. Whether the price was worth paying is a question that in a mundane sense must be left to the British democracy to settle.

At this point it may be convenient to bring in a little personal reminiscence. People sometimes ask me: 'Do you know Mrs Thatcher well?' The answer must be: 'I know her. She has always been friendly to me, but I cannot be said to know her well.' Until she became Prime Minister, she was living in the next street to us in Chelsea and at Lamberhurst, a few miles from us in Hurst Green. I well remember calling in at our newsagents in Chelsea on the Saturday morning when Mr Heath was forming his Cabinet in 1970. I ran into Margaret Thatcher, whom I already knew slightly. 'It must be an anxious day for you,' I suggested. 'Not at all,' said the potential Cabinet Minister, 'I am not the sort who hangs around the telephone.' 'Quite,' I went on, a shade insensitively, 'but I have been through all this myself, and one has to be accessible, if you are wanted.' The future Cabinet Minister melted slightly. 'Oh! that's an easy one. You get someone else to sit by the telephone!' Margaret Thatcher endeared herself to me at that moment.

Later she came to dinner in the country. She remarked of another female politician that she was a very nice woman, but 'she lacked the power of decision'. I realized from then on that that was where Margaret Thatcher considered, not unreasonably, that her own strength resided.

Denis has been caricatured on the grand scale in *Private Eye* and in a theatrical production. He has taken it calmly, but agrees with me that one doesn't see the joke of that sort of satire about oneself. Certainly the *Private Eye* 'Letters' of Denis make him out a bit of an ass, which is far from the case. He said to me *à propos* the theatrical production, which he and Margaret Thatcher attended: 'No, I can't say I enjoyed it, but I did enjoy raising twenty thousand pounds for our charities.' He and I have in common a great love of rugby football. Denis was a leading rugby referee for many years.

I had one long interview with Margaret Thatcher at the end of 1982. I had written something about her which she did not seem to think too unfair. She did not comment on it, except to say that I made her out rather like a Methodist missionary. Having been brought up as a Methodist, she may not have minded this. She tackled me quite severely about my suggestion, or implication, that anyone who interfered with the Welfare State showed a lack of compassion. In my draft, and in the House of Lords, I had spoken of her attachment to St Francis. I sent her my book about him after she declaimed his prayer for peace on becoming Prime Minister. She wrote back to say that he had always been one of her favourite saints. I was also aware, although I did not mention it, that on one occasion last year she had said this of compassion: 'It always seems to me so patronizing a word.' A remark which could be understood to illustrate her sense of the dignity of fellow-humans, her desire not to look down on them. One can't imagine that she would welcome pity directed towards herself. Now she 'ticked me off' in a friendly, intimate kind of way, in the manner of my former family governess, for suggesting that she herself was guilty of any lack of compassion towards the poor.

The argument raged vigorously. I said that I was there to listen rather than hold forth, but I obtained her permission to counter-attack on occasion which she seemed to enjoy (we are both fast talkers!). On that morning (16 October 1982) Sir John Hoskyns, her former economic adviser, spelt out at some length in *The Times* more than one of the main points she was making:

> As ever, those who question any aspect of the Welfare State are assumed to be less concerned about human suffering than those who defend it. No one is proposing that the state disowns responsibility for those who genuinely cannot help themselves. The question is whether the state should also provide large amounts of goods and services 'free' for all and sundry.

When Mrs Thatcher argued on those lines to me I submitted this was a middle- or upper-class point of view — that the great mass of the people could not help themselves to anything like the extent that the Welfare State helped them. No doubt in the end a balance will be struck in Britain between the claims of compassion, as I understand it, and self-help, a virtue not to be derided. In the present age, she no doubt feels that self-help is the more neglected quality.

We have heard at different moments about various kinds of society — the permissive society, the civilized society, the compassionate society, to name only three. My own label (not hers) for her society would be 'a deserving society'. The England she would like to see is one where everyone is rewarded according to their merits. Everyone, that is, except those so afflicted, avoidably or unavoidably, that they need special assistance. She assumes that the vast majority of us will benefit by feeling 'It's up to me, not the State.' She believes that this will make us better people and will produce a better country.

On the economic side there is room for unlimited argument as to whether *her* policies have or have not been successful. The most scathing indictment ever delivered by a Prime Minister of the economic policies of his successor was that of Mr Heath on 17 January, already referred to.

> Britain [he said] has suffered a recession deeper than any of her OECD partners. This has been due in part to policies deliberately pursued by the Government. The Government's early concern with monetarism

was naive and simplistic but the most revolutionary feature of economic policy has been the decision to give inflation priority over unemployment . . .

And much else of deadly criticism followed. On the same day the *Guardian* was attacking from a different quarter. They quoted the bold statement of the Prime Minister at her adoption meeting of 11 April 1979 that 'taxes must and taxes will come down'. The gist of their criticism was contained in their description of Britain as 'the nation where taxes rose fastest'. By the time this book appears Mrs Thatcher's economic policies may or may not be popular. At the time of writing there is considerable discussion as to whether Thatcherism is being abandoned. I would feel rather that she has begun to recognize its limits.

Myself I keep harking back to the question of how we equate her favourite saint, St Francis, with over 3 million unemployed. She is undoubtedly a great simplifier and, if only for that reason, a superb war leader if the cause is felt to be just by the vast majority of the people. Churchill was also a great simplifier. It was not difficult to simplify the cause of resisting Hitler. On a smaller scale she stirred the same feelings of patriotism which he had aroused forty years earlier, even though national pride and not national security was this time the basic issue. But, as mentioned earlier, Churchill by 1947 was already talking to me of the plight of Germany and considering how to bring her back into the comity of nations. There are few signs yet of any such flexibility on the part of Mrs Thatcher. She has, if one may use the word respectfully, a linear mind. Wellington was once asked by one of his officials, 'Which way do we go, my lord?' Wellington replied, 'Why, straight ahead, of course.' That is Mrs Thatcher's instinctive response, and she derives no small pleasure from the confrontation that follows. But she stands on a different footing from the other ten Prime Ministers. This is nothing to do with her being a woman. In assessing them one is trying to write recent history. She has already made history, but unlike them she has an unpredictable future in front of her. Cardinal Newman said that to live is to change, and to be perfect is to have changed often. At the moment one must assume that she is determined to win the next election, as it is only right and proper that she should. What effect this will have on what have hitherto been presented as inflexible principles no one can forecast with absolute certainty.

In this book I must measure her on her showing up to the present time. Life is more complicated than Margaret Thatcher has cared to admit. It is by no means easy on all occasions to know what is right and what is wrong, and one may well have to change one's course of action when more facts are available. When her much-valued Minister, Mr Parkinson, broke the news to her of his painful situation, one assumes that her first instinct was to back her admired protégé and that she declined to consider the complications and implications involved. She took a stand which has not assisted her emphasis on moral values. But much will always be forgiven to anyone to whom loyalty means as much as it does to her.

Almost every day I visit a youth centre for homeless young people, usually unemployed, which I helped to found fifteen years ago. We are now seeing about 3,500 of them in a year. Their prospects and conditions generally are not a credit to our wealthy society, whatever government is in power. But there is no doubt whatever that their plight has been made worse by the policies in which Mrs Thatcher and those who think like her so sincerely believe, and which have been pursued in the last few years. The only reply can be that those are the policies and the only policies which can benefit the whole community, including the young and disadvantaged in the long run. To quote a leading article in *The Times* (1979), which after many years remains in my mind: 'Unfortunately wealth is like heat. It is only when it is unequally distributed that it performs what the physicists call work.' A recent article in the same paper makes the same point just as dogmatically.

I am perfectly well aware that intelligent, public-spirited persons can believe implicitly in that proposition which involves the gap between the rich and the poor expanding steadily. I believed it once, but for half a century I have been unable to find any evidence to support it. For me, a Christian answer must lie elsewhere.

The Summing-Up

The Summing-Up

'THE QUESTION IS "qua mente?"' ('with what intention?'), to quote the opening words of a once famous book, *The Lost Dominion*. 'And all these men' responsible for the loss of India 'had noble ideals'. I will say the same of our eleven Prime Ministers without the implication that their performance was, on balance, a failure. But another quotation, already made use of, is ineluctable. The German Chancellor Von Bülow delivered the pronouncement: 'Real politicians are animated by two motives only – love of country and love of power.' None of our eleven notables was devoid of a considerable personal ambition, though Attlee and Home, whose rise to the top was much assisted by accident, could not be called ambitious men. Nor indeed for most of his life could this be said of Stanley Baldwin.

Ambition has not had a good press over the centuries, particularly among Christian commentators. The most famous of all sayings about ambition is that of Cardinal Wolsey: 'Cromwell, I charge thee, fling away ambition.' Ambition in the ordinary sense does not harmonize easily with the instructions in the Sermon on the Mount to be meek and poor in spirit. But there is a different emphasis in other parts of the gospels. The parable of the talents leaves one under the impression that to neglect one's gifts and opportunities is slack and sinful. Cardinal Hume tells us in his spiritual notebook *To Be a Pilgrim* that 'Only one thing matters and that is what God thinks about me. To be high in His regard is the biggest *ambition* any person can have.' The kind of ambition he refers to there is far removed from the ambition to be Prime Minister. But I am sure that Cardinal Hume when Abbot of Ampleforth, and subsequently, would never have discouraged a young man who thirsted for public achievement.

A sharp line can be drawn between our first seven and our last four. The first seven began life a long way up the 'greasy pole'; the last four had to fight hard throughout from a position a long way down. Churchill, son of a Chancellor of the Exchequer and the nephew of a duke, went to Harrow, as did Baldwin. They both sent their sons to Eton. Eden, Macmillan and Home went to Eton themselves and sent their sons there. Chamberlain did not go to Eton but to Rugby; his father, however, Joseph Chamberlain, was one of the half-dozen most important men in the country, and the Chamberlains ruled Birmingham as a family preserve. Attlee was somewhat less advantaged than the others, but he went to Haileybury and to Oxford without any kind of scholarship. His father was an eminent solicitor, at one time President of the Law Society.

The last four on our list are in a different category. All of them started life in what is broadly called the lower middle class. There were large differences between the final status of some of their parents. The mother of James Callaghan remained a petty officer's widow struggling to make both ends meet. The father of Margaret Thatcher, known to the world by now as a grocer, became Mayor of Grantham. In each case, however, the odds against the child arriving at Oxford were heavy, and against finishing at No. 10 Downing Street overwhelming. Harold Wilson, Ted Heath and Margaret Thatcher accomplished both feats. James Callaghan, more remarkably, the second without the first.

It is not quite clear to me why Callaghan left school at sixteen. One would have thought that his talents would already have been notice-able. The simple explanation appears to be that his mother, living on a small pension in South Wales, was desperately anxious to see her son secure for life. The Civil Service (even the humbler grade than that entered by university graduates) would provide perfect security throughout his working life, with a nice little pension at the end of it. Jim Callaghan, at all times a dutiful son, was guided away from school before his remarkable gifts could show themselves.

By the time he emerged from the Navy in 1945 he was a most accomplished speaker with a fine command of the English language. My friend Evan Durbin, his Labour colleague in the House of Commons and an acute judge of public speaking, told me that Jim Callaghan was the best speaker among the new entry – which included, it will be recalled, Hugh Gaitskell and Dick Crossman. Unlike Ted Heath and Margaret Thatcher, he had not needed to alter his accent upward or, like Harold Wilson, to move it downward on occasion. Jim Callaghan is notably classless: as much at home at a TUC conference as at Nuffield College, in which respect he has an advantage over all our other Prime Ministers.

Only God is able to judge the precise quality or quantity of the ambition driving our leaders forward. It must be assumed that in most cases the prospect of becoming Prime Minister was not apparent until quite late in the day. It can hardly have crossed the mind of Baldwin a year before he found himself at No. 10 through the death of Bonar Law. Churchill had striven for the first place from boyhood, but in the summer of 1939 it must still have seemed a long way off. Attlee before the Labour collapse of 1931 was hardly mentioned in Beatrice Webb's diary. Even after he became leader in 1935 through the resignation of Lansbury it was widely expected that he would be superseded by more powerful figures in the party. In any case, the chance of a Labour Government was still remote. Till the collapse of Eden, Macmillan seemed to have no chance at all of being Prime Minister, and was talking openly of retirement to the Lords. Home, a few months before he became Prime Minister, was tucked away in the Upper House and not lifting a finger to liberate himself. Wilson had no chance whatever of being Prime Minister till the death of Hugh Gaitskell in February 1963. By the autumn of the following year he had achieved supreme power.

In the struggle for the Conservative leadership in autumn 1963 Heath was not one of the first five contenders. Eighteen months later he was Leader of the Conservative Opposition. Callaghan may or may not have had some inkling that Wilson was going to retire in spring 1976. To the outside world it was a complete surprise. Margaret Thatcher was quite low in the pecking order of the Heath Cabinet and the Shadow Cabinet thereafter. Almost overnight she was leader of the party. Chamberlain and Eden are a different story. In each case there was a long period of loyal waiting in the ante-room, which in the case of Eden may well have contributed to his breakdown later.

It follows from the above that Prime Ministers have seldom reached the highest position by a persistent and well-planned campaign spread over many years to achieve that objective. Once arrived there, however, they have not given up easily. Baldwin headed off more than one venomous assault. Chamberlain missed a good opportunity to resign the premiership when war broke out or soon afterwards. It should have been plain to him that he was no longer suited for the position. Attlee was lucky to have Ernest Bevin at his elbow when Herbert Morrison challenged his right to become Prime Minister immediately after the General Election of 1945, and again when several leading colleagues conspired against him.

He was not a man who lightly deserted his post or renounced his rights, though the least self-seeking of human beings. I well remember a scene in the House of Lords when he was approaching his end. A place was kept for him by common consent – the first below the gangway. Once he was rather late. His place was taken by a bulky ex-Minister. Attlee, so frail by that time that he seemed more spirit than body, stood quietly in front of the ex-Minister for what seemed an eternity. Then the intruder shifted along.

Eden fought till he dropped. Macmillan, usually so decisive, could not bring himself to decide on retirement until the issue was taken out of his hands by the need for a sudden operation. Some years later, we are told, he considered seriously a return at the head of a coalition. The painful reluctance of Ted Heath to come to terms with Margaret Thatcher, who had supplanted him, points to a profound disturbance of mind over his supersession.

The problem has not yet arisen for Margaret Thatcher herself. The one leader of a party in our period who gave up, as I would think rather too easily, is Alec Home. Is it a coincidence that he was probably the most avowedly religious? His readiness to serve Heath in an exalted but lower capacity demonstrates that it was no lack of 'guts' which led to his withdrawal. Jim Callaghan retired after an election defeat; at sixty-four he could not expect to lead the party in another General Election. I conclude that our political leaders have been men of resolution well able to take care of themselves in the political rough and tumble. But with the exception of Churchill they were not imbued with a conviction that the first place was the only one appropriate for them.

What of their mental abilities? On any test outside that of professional politics they would make a respectable but hardly a distinguished showing. Churchill was the one man of genius among them, although he was compelled to leave Harrow in order to cram for Sandhurst. It was only at the third attempt that he succeeded in entering the latter academy. Chamberlain and Callaghan were the other two Prime Ministers who did not go to university. Chamberlain had showed very moderate abilities at Rugby. His elder brother Austen was destined for success in politics. It was hoped that Chamberlain would prosper in business. This turned out a true estimate in the long run, though his beginnings in the West Indies were disastrous.

Callaghan, as just mentioned, left school at sixteen to satisfy his mother's desire for his security. One must suppose that if he had shown exceptional promise his schoolmasters would have prevailed on her to let him proceed further with his studies.

Of the other eight, seven went to Oxford and one, Baldwin, to Cambridge. Wilson got an outstanding First at Oxford. Macmillan got a First in Honour Mods, and might well have achieved a First in Greats if he had taken them. Eden got a First in Oriental Languages. He was an admirable linguist, but not thought of at any time as an academic 'flier'. Attlee, Heath and Margaret Thatcher all got seconds. Baldwin and Home got Thirds. Leaving out the incomparable Churchill, the average result might be that of a good set of barrister's chambers. Hardly better.

But comparisons of this kind do not carry us very far. It would be a dull world if no one developed after twenty-one or if everyone developed at the same pace.

In the last resort these Prime Ministers were not selected and sustained in power for years because they were the cleverest, or even the most morally elevated. Life-style no doubt has weighed heavily. Not long ago a well-known football manager emerged in the news with a somewhat lurid private life. The chairman of the club was urged to dismiss him, but replied, 'When we hired him we didn't think that we were hiring a Sunday school teacher.' Personal virtue counts for more than that at the top of politics. On the other hand, the time has gone by when we demand, like Aristotle, that our rulers should exhibit moral virtues denied to the rest of us.

The Prime Ministers were chosen because the selectors (in the widest sense) considered that these individuals had the all-round capacity to do the job better than anyone else. The leader of a party has ideally to combine the qualities of a commander-in-chief, a chief of staff and a front-line company commander. He has to provide widespread inspiration and tactical and strategic foresight. He has to perform, above all to speak effectively, under daily conditions of extreme tension public and private. Minimum requirements are robust health, and dogged determination.

In peacetime it is incredibly difficult to provide at the same time great party and great national leadership. Baldwin managed it on occasion; Churchill from 1940 to 1945; Mrs Thatcher for a brief moment during the Falklands War, about which I myself was no kind of enthusiast. In a quieter way Attlee achieved the results he was seeking with a wide measure of national approval. Under the headings of strategic foresight and day-to-day operation my assessments should have emerged from the foregoing essays. But there is a question here worth dwelling on.

Sir John Hackett, in his brilliant book *The Profession of Arms*, suggests that military leaders at all levels are chosen or should be chosen for their superior qualities. Most of us, he says, feel our inadequacy especially under the stress of war. We desire to be led by people more adequate than ourselves on whom we can lay our burdens. Is the same true of politics?

In a democratic age, is it not rather to be assumed that the electorate will cast their votes in favour of those with whom they can identify most easily, men and women not *superior* to themselves but *like* themselves? No doubt there has been a trend in this direction. Of the nine Prime Ministers since the war, as remarked above, only two, Churchill and Callaghan, had not been to Oxford. As I suggested in the essay concerning Callaghan, this may mean that he understands the mass of the electorate all the better on that account. It may be that the electorate identify themselves with him all the more easily.

What difference in the end did our eleven make individually or collectively? Would the course of British or for that matter world history have been other than it was if different individuals had resided in No. 10 during the last half-century?

I was speaking to a distinguished Ambassador recently retired about this same half-century, and he remarked unhappily, 'It's sad to think that for Britain this has been a period of unrelieved decline.' I cannot share that amount of gloom. From the point of view of British influence, diplomatic prestige, the proposition is arguably true. Fifty years ago the destiny of the world seemed to depend on how Britain and France behaved towards Germany. Today we live in an age of the two super-powers and a United Nations, where we are told that 140 out of the 157 states are non-democratic. We live in an age where an Empire covering a quarter of the globe has been succeeded by a Commonwealth over which we do not seek to have much or any control. It is not to be expected that Britain, a small island of 50-odd million inhabitants, should be as dominant as in the good old days.

On the other hand, we live in an age where the standard of life, especially among the poorer sections of the community, is many times higher, partly through an all-round increase in wealth, partly through an improved distribution. Fifty years ago the old-age pension was ten shillings a week. The treatment of the unemployed is altogether more humane, though at the moment the number of them is as shocking as it was in the 1930s, more shocking in view of the lessons that ought to have been learnt. In other words, the Welfare State represents a social advance of incalculable benefit.

But along with the Welfare State has gone the permissive society, although there is no necessary connection between the two. And here the losses are more obvious than the gains. The escalating figures for divorce, illegitimate births and abortion are matched by a remorseless increase in crime. In this latter area it is impossible to give any particular credit to our Prime Ministers or any particular blame except, if we are judging them harshly, for sins of omission. The outcasts with whom I have been much concerned in recent years – the mentally disordered and prisoners, for example – can thank our individual Prime Ministers about as much as they can thank the average Member of Parliament, which is a very limited testimonial. Mrs Thatcher continues, it seems, to support capital punishment, a horrifying thought. On the other hand, she has emerged more bravely than any other leading politician of recent times in support of Mary Whitehouse and her indomitable struggle against pornography.

What of the policies pursued? Of our group of eleven, eight were Conservatives – Baldwin, Chamberlain, Churchill, Eden, Macmillan, Home, Heath, Margaret Thatcher; three were Labour – Attlee, Wilson, Callaghan. The difference between dry and wet, hard and soft, reactionary and progressive Conservatives has been high-lighted in the last few years. It was not evident pre-war. In domestic affairs Harold Macmillan was the only Tory who broke away to the left of his party. During the war, sectional differences were muted. To follow the war there was a general desire for a more just and humanitarian society. Churchill, with the excuse of overwhelming wartime duties, showed himself noticeably indifferent to proposals such as those of Sir William Beveridge. When he returned to office in 1951 he showed little interest in social policy. Eden and Home were specialists in foreign affairs.

Macmillan, however, never forgot the unemployed in Stockton in the 1930s. He was favourable at all times to expansion. Chancellors of the Exchequer like Thorneycroft and Selwyn Lloyd, who reflected the restrictionism associated with the Treasury, found themselves on the sidelines. Heath moved from restrictionism to expansion. He was undone by the 1973 oil crisis, the three-day week and the miners' strike. Margaret Thatcher introduced policies quite different from those of her post-war predecessors, Conservative or Labour. Neville Chamberlain would have approved.

The three Labour Prime Ministers, Attlee, Wilson and Callaghan, were all moderate socialists and, in Labour terms, right wing (though they all claimed to be left of centre by the time they arrived at Downing Street). Attlee achieved the most peaceful of social revolutions. Wilson and Callaghan left much less mark, though they never ceased to strive actively for social justice. It is fair to point out that Attlee till 1950 had a large majority. Wilson from 1964 to 1966 and from 1974 to 1976, Callaghan from 1976 to 1979, had no majority of significance. Wilson had on paper a good opportunity from 1966 to 1970, but by that time the problem of restraining wage demands without a strong incomes policy had arisen to thwart his purposes, as it did those of Heath and Callaghan. It was left to Mrs Thatcher to confront the trades unions with the help of a policy of deflation and the grim fact of 3 million unemployed. There has been a renewed emphasis on 'Victorian values', the moral quality of self-help and the economic benefits of traditional private enterprise. While this book is going to press there is considerable discussion as to whether Thatcherism will be modified in the immediate future. There are no grounds yet for saying so with confidence.

In foreign affairs the picture before the war was complicated by the existence of several conflicting policies. The main ones were those of Chamberlain (appeasement), Churchill (rapid rearmament and defiance of the dictators) and Attlee, Leader of the Labour Party (firm resistance to the dictators, but reliance placed on collective security). Eden and his friends stood for a somewhat more idealistic version of Churchill's policy. To the left of the official Labour Party were communists, fellow-travellers and various kinds of pacifists. The Liberals can claim with some plausibility that they combined the best elements in the attitudes of the other parties. The ranks closed during the war in the national struggle for survival.

Since the war, the mainlines of British foreign policy have been little affected by the nature of the party in power. 'I am glad that my friend, Ernest Bevin, is going to the Foreign Office,' said Churchill in 1945. 'He'll roll all over the map of Europe, but at least he's against the communists.' The Atlantic Alliance initiated by Attlee and Bevin on the British side has been the backbone of British foreign and defence policy for thirty-five years, alike under Labour and Conservative governments. The horrendous development of nuclear weapons has not yet affected the fundamentals although increasing the demand here and elsewhere for a multilateral disarmament. The unilateralists have become more and more prominent. The General Election of 1983 demonstrated the present limits of their influence.

At the moment of writing the Labour Party is proposing an attitude to armaments and nuclear weapons in particular that is in sharp contrast to that of the Conservatives and to that which they have themselves pursued when in office. Callaghan, Labour Prime Minister from 1976 to 1979, was booed at the 1983 Labour Party Conference. However, his Chancellor of the Exchequer, Denis Healey, is still the Labour Party foreign affairs spokesman and does not admit to any change of view. It is too early to say how Labour would actually perform in office. Personally I do not believe that any government will be elected in Britain which does not convince the public that it will play its part in an adequate defence system.

A supreme disappointment for all who hoped to build a new and more peaceful world society has been the failure of any system of collective security to emerge through the United Nations. Labour would probably have gone further down that way than the Tories, but Russian intransigence has stultified progress from the first. No one worth his salt in politics despairs of arms control, but at the time of writing no light is showing. As against that, the emergence of the European Economic Community and our own inclusion in it are blessings, which no one forecast at the end of the war. No one party can take the credit or the blame here, but Edward Heath is the name which should receive special honour.

Our attitude to the shocking poverty of the Third World is a sorry tale. Harold Wilson, however, and Ted Heath, after he ceased to be Prime Minister, have shown a genuine commitment.

What of the personal responsibility for achievement or the lack of it? It is impossible not to blame Baldwin and Chamberlain for British foreign policy in the years from 1931 to 1939, though Baldwin was not Prime Minister (for the third time) until 1935. Lord Home, in his *Letters to a Grandson*, provides a partial defence by calling attention to British public opinion at that time. To put it another way, no British Prime Minister who could have been chosen during those years would have done much better. There was no chance of Churchill being called to the helm until the worst occurred. Nevertheless, some degree of failure remains.

We can agree unequivocally that Winston Churchill made the whole difference to the survival of Britain and the freedom of the world in 1940. If he had not been swept into the leadership at that time it is possible – probable, perhaps – that we should either have made a negotiated peace or been defeated. Here is one instance at least where a single man has crucially affected the course of history.

Attlee achieved almost as much in the most unobtrusive manner possible. He presided over the establishment of the Welfare State with the minimum of fuss and provocation. He initiated the movement from Empire to Commonwealth. He emancipated India so wisely and tactfully that she agreed to remain in the Commonwealth. He and Bevin laid the foundations of the Atlantic Alliance which has been the basis of British and Western defence since that time. I question whether any one English statesman has ever achieved so much in peacetime.

Eden will be remembered for much wise diplomacy when he was Foreign Secretary. The best that can be said for the Suez adventure is that it led us to reconsider our imperial position, with ultimate benefit. Macmillan, by his personal exertions, re-established Britain's position in the world, and in particular our friendship with the United States. His passionate desire to avoid the unemployment of the 1930s led him to carry on the ideas of John Maynard Keynes when other Tory leaders might have discarded them. But

R. A. Butler, the alternative, would almost certainly have acted like Macmillan.

Lord Home was Prime Minister for too short a time to leave much mark in that capacity. As Foreign Secretary before and after his premiership, he stood for an unyielding, though never provocative, resistance to Soviet communism. Harold Wilson led the Labour Party for thirteen years. He was Prime Minister first for six years and then for two. It is a simple fact that he held the party together by skilful management. Whether under Hugh Gaitskell, with his firmer emphasis on principles, the task would have been accomplished so harmoniously or accomplished at all must remain a matter of guesswork.

Ted Heath comes between the two Wilson periods of government. His suspension of Stormont and his promotion of the Sunningdale Agreement represent a noble effort to solve the horrendous problems of Northern Ireland. He is entitled to feel that if he had not been defeated at the 1974 election (but the decision to call that election was his own) he might have turned the Sunningdale Agreement into a triumphant success. In the event it was sabotaged by the Ulster workers' strike. Heath will always be remembered for negotiating and carrying through Parliament the British entry into the European Economic Community. He will be recalled less favourably for his unsuccessful showdown with the miners and for fighting and losing an election during the three-day week.

Till about 1970 things were made relatively easy in Britain by steady economic growth throughout the world. From 1970 – that is, from about the time when Heath came to power and still more from 1973 after the oil crisis – the world situation deteriorated and British difficulties increased accordingly. The expectations of the workers, the assumption that higher standards of living would be available year by year, continued unabated. Heath during this period, Wilson in 1974–6 and Callaghan in 1976–9 found themselves in deeper and deeper trouble through no personal inferiority to their predecessors. None of our post-war Prime Ministers had faced up successfully to the problem of how to combine full employment and reasonably stable prices; though for a long time world conditions concealed the gravity of the issue. It was not surprising that a new type of policy should appeal to the Conservatives. That is not to say that if Mrs Thatcher had not existed it would have been necessary to invent her. It does not by any means follow that there would have been Thatcherism without Margaret Thatcher.

Those who feel that Britain has steadily declined in the last fifty years, apart from the years of wartime glory, will place no small measure of blame on our political leaders. But by any historical standards the establishment of the Welfare State, the emancipation of the Commonwealth and the foundation of the Atlantic Alliance were all splendid achievements. Our belated entry into Europe is also a reason for much satisfaction. So has been the large improvement in the all-round standard of life and the considerable redistribution of wealth. The standard of life has continued to improve, though more sluggishly in recent times. In other respects, the last thirty years are as notable for unpleasant as for pleasant features, especially the increase in crime. In a study of our political leaders, one cannot fail to mention the ever-stronger moral inspiration supplied by the present Queen.

Our Prime Ministers have not been, do not aspire to be and must not be expected to be super-persons. The Prime Ministers who covered the preceding years of the century were Salisbury, Balfour, Asquith, Lloyd George, Bonar Law and MacDonald (who overlapped with Baldwin). In my reckoning Salisbury and Balfour were too élitist; Asquith and Lloyd George too unsatisfactory in their private lives; Bonar Law too depressed and depressing; MacDonald, even in his prime, not quite sufficiently balanced, though I should dearly like to have met him. Our selected eleven may not, apart from Churchill, excel the others in mental endowment. But as human beings they seem to me to have been more suited to lead the nation in difficult times.

Index